AN IBM GUIDE TO DOING BUSINESS ON THE INTERNET

Kendra R. Bonnett

McGraw-Hill

New York   San Francisco   Washington, D.C.   Auckland   Bogotá
Caracas   Lisbon   London   Madrid   Mexico City   Milan
Montreal   New Delhi   San Juan   Singapore
Sydney   Tokyo   Toronto

Library of Congress Cataloging-in-Publication Data

Bonnett, Kendra.
    An IBM guide to doing business on the Internet / Kendra R. Bonnett.
    p. cm.
    ISBN 0-07-031846-8
    1. Electronic commerce. I. Title.

HF5548.32 .B66 2000
658.8′4—dc21
                                              99-086111

McGraw-Hill

A Division of The **McGraw·Hill** *Companies*

   3 4 5 6 7 8 9 0 DOC / DOC 0 9 8 7 6 5 4 3 2 1 0

ISBN 0-07-031846-8

*This book was typeset in New Times Roman by Inkwell Publishing
Services. Printed and bound by R. R. Donnelley & Sons Company.*

McGraw-Hill books are available at special quantity discounts to use
as premiums and sales promotions, or for use in corporate training
programs. For more information, please write to the Director of
Special Sales, Professional Publishing, McGraw-Hill, Two Penn
Plaza, New York, NY 10121-2298. Or contact your local bookstore.

This book is printed on recycled, acid-free paper
containing a minimum of 50% recycled de-inked fiber.

CONTENTS

PREFACE

As we enter the new millennium, we find ourselves questioning, redefining, and wondering: What will the years ahead bring? How will new technology enhance or change our lives? In what new ways will we rely on computers in our homes and offices? With the dramatic and accelerating growth of the Internet, we must include the impact of the Internet, and particularly the World Wide Web, in any discussions or plans for our business and personal activities.

We need to be careful, however, not to allow the technology per se to overtake the more critical issue of what we will do with it. We can assume that connections will become faster, Web sites richer in content, and applications for conducting business more inclusive. How we will apply these advantages is less obvious, and leads to the critical question each business owner must ask: How can we develop our Web sites to make them as useful and effective as possible? In speaking before the Organization for Economic Cooperation and Development Ministerial Conference in Ottawa (October 8, 1998), IBM CEO Louis V. Gerstner, Jr. explained: "...the Net is about business, not browsing; and about conducting real commerce, not merely accessing a bottomless reservoir of content." In other words, the Internet is more than a catchall for information. It is a tool that maintains the information and systems that will help us work more effectively.

The challenge before every business owner is how to create a Web site that facilitates business within and outside the organization. To do this, we need to anticipate the online market, understand how we can apply those trends to meet our business objectives, and determine the most effective way to present our online capability to customers and employees. One thing we know is that online business efforts will require new models that factor in customer and employee wants and needs as well as business objectives. Again, Gerstner expressed the imperative we all face: "...the real revolution is not about the technology. The revolution is about the changes in institutional processes that must take place to seize the advantage of the network." (Second International Harvard Conference on the Internet and Society, May 27, 1998.)

One of the possibilities we must consider is that retail commerce as we know it today could disappear. Shopping malls may someday be abandoned for the convenience of shopping online. Local retailers may feel compelled to rely on a global market for survival. And start-up businesses may attract millions of customers in a matter of months. None of these visions is all that far-fetched. Someday business could become nothing but Net...Internet, that is.

While it's impossible to say just what will happen and when, we can be certain that *e-commerce*—the capacity to conduct business transactions online—will forever change how we shop. Even more dramatic will be the lasting impact of *e-business*, which encompasses any and all aspects of business conducted online, including administration, management, and operations.

If you don't believe this, consider the evidence. To start, you need look no further than the reports that appear in the news every day. In early 1998, for example, the computer and software retailer Egghead Inc. became the first major retail chain to close all of its stores in favor of one big store in cyberspace. CEO George Orban decided that the company's survival depended on closing its last 80 outlets across the country (vestiges of a retail chain that was once more than 200 strong) and doing business exclusively over the Internet, as Egghead.com. The online bookstore Amazon.com, which did not exist outside the imagination of its founder five years ago, now has customers numbering in the millions and revenues in the hundreds of millions of dollars. And America Online, unknown 15 years ago, went public in 1995; four years later its stock was considered significant enough to be included in the leading index of the Standard and Poor's 500. With events like these being reported daily, we have to acknowledge that the very fiber of business is changing—and changing permanently.

The impact of the Internet and the World Wide Web requires all business owners, and perhaps most especially small business owners, to rethink their opportunities. With the help of the Internet, today's small business owners have greater potential than ever before to:

• Expand their businesses far outside their present boundaries.

• Build a customer and prospect base that numbers in the millions.

• Provide a much higher and more personal level of customer service without increasing the size of the service department proportionately.

• Grow their businesses with a smaller capital investment in brick-and-mortar buildings, personnel, and inventory than traditional businesses had to make.

Perhaps it is a little surprising, given the prospect of such expanding possibilities, that the majority of small businesses are still on the sidelines. The Yankee Group reports that only 31 percent of small businesses and 51 percent of medium businesses surveyed believe that the Internet is "important to achieving business goals." Furthermore, among the businesses without an online presence, 55 percent of small and 66 percent of medium businesses have no current plans to bring their businesses online. Cahners In-Stat Group reports that only 28 percent of those small businesses conducting some form of e-business actually support online ordering; only 19 percent accept payments directly over the Internet. The In-Stat Group found that the most often-cited reasons for not acting are the cost of creating a Web site and concern for online security.

Nothing but Net? Perhaps not...or at least not for several years. But consider the rate of growth of Web pages: In 1998, the Internet was made up of slightly fewer than 1 billion pages. By the end of 1999, the United States Internet Council expected that number to grow to almost 1.5 billion;

by 2000, to close to 2.7 billion; and by 2002, to more than 7.5 billion pages. Every business owner who expects to thrive, or even survive, in the twenty-first century must take careful stock of his or her opportunities today. This means overcoming any stumbling blocks, including cost and security issues, and weighing these concerns against the potential opportunity. International Data Corporation (IDC) finds that, as a group, small businesses that use the Internet have higher revenues than those that do not ($3.79 million compared with $2.72 million). Furthermore, iCat Corporation (a division of Intel Corporation) finds that 81 percent of business owners surveyed expect that online sales will boost their total annual revenues by between 15 percent and 50 percent. The drive is on, at least among those with vision.

What makes all this more intriguing is the speed with which e-business has taken root. In 1994, IBM sponsored Roper Starch Worldwide Inc. to survey more than 500 small business executives for their perceptions of the Internet (then commonly referred to as the Information Highway). Slightly more than half of the respondents had not heard the phrase "Information Highway." Among that 52 percent, only 3 percent felt that they knew a lot about it. Furthermore, 45 percent of all respondents believed it would take between 6 and 15 years for the Internet to "become a reality for 50 percent of small businesses" in the United States.

The rate of change has been much faster. Consider this statement from an April 15, 1998, Associated Press release: "It took 38 years before radio had 50 million listeners and television took 13 years to reach that mark. The Internet crossed the line in just four years." The United States Internet Council (www.usic.org) further confirms the Internet's rapid rate of acceptance: The Internet reached 30 percent of the U.S. population in just seven years. This rate overshadows the rate of acceptance of all other technologies. For computers to reach 30 percent of people in the United States took 13 years; television 17 years; and telephones 38 years. In that time, the ubiquitous "dot com" has become a familiar phrase—one that holds the potential to broaden consumer and business-to-business opportunities on a scale never before imagined, especially among small firms.

International Data Corporation finds that among businesses with fewer than ten employees, the interest in e-mail and the Internet is affecting expenditures on information technology. As a result, they were expected to spend $55.9 billion in 1999, and by 2002 that amount is estimated to grow to more than $70 billion.

The little "e" is changing everything. Terms like e-commerce, e-business, and e-tailing, and even new concepts like portals, cybermalls, and virtual retail can seem confusing and complex—and completely beyond reach. They should also drive you to challenge the status quo as it relates to your business and suggest the questions that will help carry your business into the twenty-first century: How are we going to use the Web to bring additional value to our businesses? Can we really expect to expand outside our current boundaries? How are we going to weave this new medium into the existing fabric of our businesses?

An IBM Guide to Doing Business on the Internet will help you develop the skills you need to take your business online, or to build upon what you have already started. It will help prepare you to make the decisions that are critical to your success—and ultimately to your survival.

Although the technology behind the Internet is important, you have access to Web design tools, services, and professional developers that makes it increasingly easy and cost-effective to have a Web presence. This frees you to focus on the bigger (and more important) task: building a strategic and tactical model that factors the appropriate Web presence into the totality of your business.

This guide provides a thoughtful, creative look at where the Internet fits into companies' overall sales, marketing, communications, and customer service strategies for the twenty-first century. As a handbook for developing the strategic tools and skill sets to leverage the Internet for sales, lead generation, brand exposure, competitive research, public relations, and more, it will help you build an effective business model. You'll learn how to:

- Leverage your marketing investment.
- Increase exposure and drive business through the Internet.
- Close business and get hot leads online.

- Create a global market for your products and services.
- Increase your Internet visibility.
- Attract repeat visitors to your Web site.
- Communicate effectively with customers, suppliers, partners, and employees.

The advice, tips, and worksheets included in this book were distilled from 1) studying some of the best examples of successful Web sites among businesses small and large, and 2) gathering, through interviews, the first-hand experiences of business owners, Web site developers, and industry experts. Many of those interviewed are people whose efforts have been responsible for shaping the commercial nature of the Web as we know it today. Let their creativity, marketing savvy, and willingness to keep the customer first in their minds inspire your work and, in addition, give you an insight into the realistic expectations of customers and the size of the challenge before you.

The Web is nothing to fear. It is also not to be taken lightly. Your success rests with your capacity to understand the workings and implications of the Internet and your ability to meld new ideas with the basic rules of common sense and good marketing. Your challenge is learning to apply them most effectively to a medium that is changing many of the rules. Business owners who combine common-sense marketing with firsthand familiarity of the Internet and good insight into what their prospects, customers, partners, and suppliers want will be best prepared to make the most of their business opportunities.

Remember that, while having a presence online may soon become critical to a business's success, having a plan is always imperative.

INTRODUCTION

L isten to the financial newscasters expound on the high-flying Internet stocks or to the merger and acquisition reports about which "dot com" just bought that other "dot com." While it may seem that business judgment and good common sense have taken flight, we may actually be observing the harbinger of a new millennium of business.

You don't have to look far to find stories of start-ups running their businesses exclusively on the Internet or of traditional retailers reinventing themselves online. Here are a few quick case studies:

Preview Travel (www.previewtravel.com) has been selling travel services for vacation and business since May 1996. In that time, the site has grown to 6 million registered members. Travel bookings in 1998 surpassed $200 million. The company's dramatic growth can be attributed to the quality of customer service and its early online presence. But it is the range of relationships maintained online and the site's distinctive features that really set it apart from the competition. For example, Preview's Farefinder service helps travelers find the lowest airline fares posted online. Business travel-

ers also have at hand a wide range of other tools to help them prepare for
that next trip quickly and conveniently, including: frequent traveler information (listing airline and hotel loyalty programs); maps; customs information; a currency converter; hotel, restaurant, and car finder services; and
even an online travel store to help customers pick up last-minute travel
items. In addition to building relationships with other key sites, including
America Online, Lycos, Snap, Excite, and USA Today, Preview Travel has
syndicated its Farefinder and Travel Newswire services, inviting other Web
site owners to post these tools (free of charge), thus providing broader
access to these useful tools and, Preview hopes, helping to draw new
prospects to its site.

TIP

In some cases, developing and distributing a proprietary tool or
utility provides useful information that may be more effective than
a banner ad in drawing potential new customers to your site.

Barnes and Noble (www.barnesandnoble.com) brought its years of bookselling experience online in May 1997, and in less than two years has been
recognized as the fourth largest e-commerce site. In 1998 the company
reported that 1.3 million customers from 177 countries bought books from
it online. Unlike the many online start-ups, Barnes and Noble had established inventories, distributor networks, and other relationships at its dis-
posal. Conversely, it also had to fight years of tradition, habit, and success
to look seriously at the Web as an important source of revenue. The book-
seller appears, however, to be playing an excellent game of catch-up with
Amazon.com, and today features many useful and unique resources to
make book shopping rewarding and pleasurable. Some of the features
include a list of 6.5 million out-of-print and rare books available for purchase online, magazine subscriptions, free e-mail greeting cards, collec-

tor's and signed editions, college textbooks, and a wealth of national book reviews, National Public Radio author readings, and Starbucks Coffee. While you can't get a cup of java online, you can order coffee beans and brew your own while you browse the stacks...or the categories.

TIP

If you are not the first in your industry category to go online, you'll want to apply all your creativity to ensure that yours is not seen as a "me-too" site.

Yahoo! (www.yahoo.com) has arguably been the premiere directory site for several years; it is a search engine that delivers more than entries matching a set of search criteria. It provides users with the added value of categories and evaluations of sites. Since its inception in 1994, Yahoo! has developed into a major portal (a site that serves as the primary starting point and hub for many online users), with more than 35 million registrations, and continues to attract visitors and members with its many special features. Among the offerings members can enjoy are free e-mail services; personalized MyYahoo! pages; an online calendar service; and Yahoo! Pager, which alerts members when their friends are online as well as alerting them to news, sports scores, and stock quotes. Now Yahoo! has become an online merchant. Yahoo! Store provides access to a wide range of products and services, including a feature that enables virtually anyone to set up an e-commerce site on the Yahoo! server quickly and easily. This strategy continues to pay off. Yahoo!, which is publicly traded, reported $76.4 million in revenue in the fourth quarter of 1998 (three times the same period in 1997) and annual revenue of $203.2 million. Yahoo! management estimates that visitors and members view more than 160 million pages per day on Yahoo!

TIP

Never be content with the status quo on your site. Add to the content, enhance or broaden your offerings, and provide real services. Set a schedule for these additions and stick to it.

Cyberian Outpost (www.outpost.com), founded in 1995, is another early comer online. It is designed to make shopping online for computer hardware, software, and peripherals both easy and financially prudent. Outpost.com gives customers access to reviews, research, and price checks to help them select the right product at the best price. In addition, for those who need software immediately but don't want to take a trip to the computer store, Outpost.com offers software sales and downloads of many popular packages. Customers seem to find Cyberian Outpost as cool as its stock ticker symbol (NASD: COOL). Fourth-quarter revenues reported April 1999 were $33 million, four times the same quarter in the previous year and 40 percent greater than the third quarter; the company also gained 70,000 new customers. For the fiscal year ending February 1999, Cyberian Outpost reported $85 million in revenue (33 percent greater than the previous year). The Monday after Thanksgiving 1998, the site registered its first million-dollar day.

These businesses are just the tip of the online iceberg. Don't let their successes frighten you away from cyberspace. Instead, their success should awaken you to the importance of examining your online prospects now and defining your opportunities. It's not too late. All the best ideas are not already taken, largely because the rules of business are being rewritten every day, which means the greatest ideas probably have yet to be conceived.

A case in point: Shortly after online retailers began enticing customers with deep discounts in order to build the mass visitation needed to attract advertising and other retailers to their sites (and perhaps even expand their sites to portal or destination-site status), Onsale Inc. changed the rules. This innovative, real-time, interactive auction site, started in May 1995, had enjoyed success from the first. According to president and CEO Jerry Kaplan, the site has been consistently profitable since July 1996. But in 1998, management changed the rules by offering customers new products (largely computers and electronics) at cost, plus shipping and administrative fees.

TIP

The ability of local businesses and retailers to fulfill customers' demands for instant gratification sets a standard or level of expectation you need to match or exceed. Sometimes you can use technology to meet that expectation; at other times you'll need to provide an alternative and equally compelling service.

THE INTERNET WAS MADE FOR BUSINESS

Of the more than 5 million registered domain names, more than 3 million have the "dot com" suffix, which identifies them as commercial sites (as opposed to government, educational, or organizational sites). Hambrecht & Quist notes that domain name registrations have doubled every year for the past several years. However, the firm expects the rate to increase significantly (20 times during the next 4 years). By the year 2002, Hambrecht & Quist expects there will be 32 million registered domain names.

What is especially remarkable about this fact is that the Internet was originally developed as the exclusive domain of government, educational, and scientific institutions and personnel in the early 1970s, and it remained so through most of the 1980s. The World Wide Web and commercial domains have been in existence only since the late 1980s.

Even if you plan to wait a year to put your business online, get your company and product names registered now.

The strategy appears to be paying off. Kaplan reports that customers have made more than 10 million bids since the site's inception and more than 1 million people are registered at the site. All the while, satisfaction remains high. During the fourth quarter of 1998, 77 percent of the auction bidders were repeat customers. At the same time, more and more home and business users are checking with "Onsale at Cost" before looking elsewhere to buy. Onsale's decision to offer products at cost is forcing several other retailers to consider a similar strategy. While this may sound like a traditional price war, it is really just the latest tactic in the campaign to win (and retain) high customer approval, which translates into a larger customer base and more leverage in the real war—to build online relationships and garner more advertising dollars.

LOTS OF ROOM FOR GROWTH

Even though online shopping during the 1998 and 1999 holiday seasons outstripped even the most liberal industry estimates, we need to examine the facts carefully to understand their true meaning:

- International Data Corporation in Framingham, Massachusetts, reported that as of December 20, 1999, online retailers were meeting or exceeding their holiday sales revenues.

- An IDC survey of e-tailers found that 26 percent saw holiday sales more than double, with another 23 percent experiencing 61 to 100 percent growth.

- Analysts at Zona Research Inc., a subsidiary of IntelliQuest Information Group, estimated that the average size of a sale during the 1998 holidays was $629, up 191 percent from 1997.

- For the year 1998, online revenues hit $13 billion, as reported by the Boston Consulting Group.

According to Zona/IntelliQuest research, the Internet has surpassed catalog shopping in popularity among consumers, to capture the third position behind brand-name stores (most popular) and discount retailers. Equally telling is the fact that 34 percent of online consumers admitted that when they could not find what they wanted online for the holidays, they elected not to buy at all, rather than fight the retail store crowds. There appears to be a significant portion of online shoppers who are selecting the new medium to the exclusion of others. While the Internet is putting pressure on catalogers, the catalog industry is also beginning to realize the advantages of taking its business online. The traditional software retailer, for example, is finding e-commerce slightly more cost-effective than conventional catalog sales (18 percent versus 20 percent cost of sales). Recognizing the growing significance of online retail business, the United States Commerce Department no longer lumps e-commerce statistics in with catalog sales. The numbers now stand on their own.

Now let's put these data in perspective. As healthy as the 1998 and 1999 online holiday shopping was, it still represented only about 2 percent of total (offline and online combined) holiday sales (*Source:* National Retail Federation/Deloitte & Touche). For the year 1998, the $13 billion spent online represent less than 1 percent of the U.S. Gross Domestic Product. For all the activity, clearly there is still plenty of room for growth and more than enough opportunity to go around. International Data Corporation reported that for the year 1999, online shoppers completed more than $109 billion in purchases, and predicted that that number would reach $1.3 trillion by 2003.

Forrester Research has its own assessment regarding the development of e-commerce in the United States. Its analysts believe the country has entered the "commerce threshold" phase, a term the firm uses to define the critical building period. This phase is expected to last 18 to 24 months, and to be followed by 5 to 10 years of unprecedented "hypergrowth." Forrester analysts believe it's even possible that the high-tech industries of computers and electronics have already entered the hypergrowth phase. Business owners, take heed: "The better entrepreneurs understand the Internet—its strengths and limits—the greater their ultimate success," explains Peter Rowley, IBM general manager, Global Small and Medium Business. "Those who wait may find it increasingly difficult to catch up with the competition later."

CHALLENGE: IDENTIFY YOUR BASIC OBJECTIVE

To bring your business to the World Wide Web, you need to be very clear about your objectives. There are three basic reasons for bringing your business online:

1. To sell your own products or services. The actual transaction can be handled either online or offline, but increasingly customers will expect you to offer full-service e-commerce capabilities.

2. To attract to your site large numbers of potential buyers who match a predetermined set of demographics, and then sell access to these loyal "visitors." Providing access to a well-defined critical mass of users can bring any number of advantages: advertising revenue, retail opportunities, joint ventures, and various co-marketing relationships.

3. To manage more efficiently and cost-effectively the communications, administrative, and basic operational functions that are critical to the business. These tasks fall under the category of e-business.

Note that some businesses set objectives around some combination of these three functions, but all include at least one of these elements.

1

ELEVEN CRITICAL RULES OF THE WEB

Every experienced Web user has his or her favorite Web rules by which to do business, ranging from strategies for marketing and communications to techniques for operations and creativity. The eleven rules that follow reflect my philosophy and the experience of many entrepreneurs for creating success online.

Whether you aspire to building your site into a major portal or destination site (where customers come for access to a wide range of services, including free e-mail, online calendar management, search engines, and direct links to sites of potential interest to a particular demographic group) or just want to sell your products online, you need to take steps to set your site apart from the competition and win top-of-mind status.

If you are interested in the prospect of becoming a portal, you may be encouraged by the fact that the recent IDC and Relevant Knowledge Web Trends Report found that more than 22 million home users are not yet faithful to any single portal. They move about, depending on their immediate needs and the breadth of tools and services available on a site. Many experts predict that when the dust begins to settle on the recent explosion in mergers and acquisitions, we'll be left with a handful of true portals. Perhaps your site will be one of the acquisitions; or you may find your own niche online. In either case, these rules will help you create a successful Web site. "The fact is, the Internet is making us all reevaluate our businesses," explains Julie Woods of IBM. "Being left behind is an option none of us can even contemplate. Therefore, the only path is one that incorporates those elements of e-business that make the most sense to each of our businesses. The more you understand the process, the easier your decisions will be and the better prepared you will be to spend your time and money where it will do the most good."

RULE 1: THINK OUT OF THE BOX

Be innovative. Being online is not conducting business as usual. You have the freedom and flexibility of a new medium. For example, as an online business, you don't have the same investment in brick and mortar, personnel, or even inventory that a conventional business must make. The broader the base of a traditional business, the greater the burden of these critical components. Some e-tailers never stock inventory, preferring to pass orders directly on to suppliers and distributors and take a percentage of the price for serving as the Internet Transaction Broker.

Even testing is less expensive online, which enables you to experiment more freely and frequently. Why stick to the same old business? Just as Amazon.com has branched out to videos, CDs, gifts, auctions, and now toys, you might consider doing the same. It's a matter of identifying a new product line or service, having the appropriate wholesale and distributor resources, and designing and marketing a Web site that will attract the customers most likely to purchase.

One of the classic jokes in business is that of the merchants who get into a price war with their competition and cut costs to the point where they end up losing money on every sale. The merchants, unfazed, retort, "That's all right, we'll make it up in volume." The joke, of course, is that if you are already losing money, then all you'll do by increasing volume is lose even more and go out of business that much faster. This only makes any sense in traditional business when a large volume gives you a greater discount with the manufacturer and lowers your wholesale costs.

The Internet has turned even this logic upside down. While the basic rule is still valid, some online businesses are deliberately designing business models guaranteed to lose money—at least in the early phases. To these cyber-entrepreneurs, success is measured in terms of the number of loyal customers they can document and retain. Their ability to reach and influence millions of consumer and business-to-business shoppers makes their concept compelling and their site attractive to other business owners with something to sell. This is the theory behind the portal or destination-site model. In fact, the ability to serve up customers is a strategy many business owners who expect to earn significant revenue from *sellers* are trying. The products or services a portal site sells (or gives away) in the early phases are irrelevant, except for (1) their ability to attract shoppers and regular visitors who match a predetermined demographic profile and (2) their capacity to be accepted as a business to be trusted, with products and services that people feel comfortable buying or using online. These cyber-entrepreneurs believe it's the people, not the immediate sales, who will make their businesses successful. While it's still too early to tell how many will win using this strategy, it's an excellent example of thinking out of the box.

The entrepreneurs at Free PC Inc., a Pasadena, California-based startup, have another idea. They are giving away 10,000 free desktop computers to consumers who 1) meet strict demographic criteria and 2) agree to receive targeted advertising. Their objective is to attract advertisers who want to reach their carefully chosen audience of consumers. At the time of this writing, Free PC is looking for 200 advertisers to pay $100,000 each to participate in a 90-day trial. It's too soon to know if such radical tactics will earn profits. Many still believe such models are flawed. "New ideas are easy to generate," says Jerome LoMonaco, president of New York City-based Premiere Interactive Design. "Whether or not they will work is a matter of 1) putting together the best plan you can, 2) considering as many potential situations as possible, and 3) getting out there in the market and testing the hell out of it. In the end, however, only the consumer will determine the merit of your idea." Ideas like Free PC Inc. do, however, illustrate the out-of-the-box thinking being applied to online businesses today.

CHALLENGE: RELEASE YOUR IMAGINATION

One of the great inhibitors of fresh thinking is your business. We all tend to follow the rules and time-honored axioms of our industries. It's time for you to break the ties that bind, and a sure-fire technique is to immerse yourself in the ways of other industries. Often the farther a field you go, the better. You'll be surprised how something—even the most ordinary or accepted tactic—in another field can be adapted to deliver startling new results. Free PC Inc.'s idea to give away computers—$1000 items—certainly falls into this category. Look around you, and start expanding your field of vision today.

RULE 2: ESTABLISH YOUR ONLINE BUSINESS AS A "KILLER CLICK"

A site that Web users feel compelled to bookmark is a site that receives greater return visitation. This is a killer click and one of the keys to longevity and ongoing success. If you aren't getting bookmarked, you probably haven't completely fulfilled your customers' expectations and, therefore, run the risk of being a flash in the pan, no matter how effective you are at getting visitors to your site the first time.

It is important to establish yourself as a popular site early. The fact is, customers can only be loyal to a comparative handful of sites. It will be more difficult (though certainly not impossible) to get people to abandon a site they frequent in favor of yours.

TIP

To become a "killer click," you must provide users with the tools, services, and products they want and need. And by all means, remind users to bookmark your site.

If you are in the business of building a destination site, a portal, or even a vertical community online, you need to be among the first sites your target audience visits each time they log on. This will help increase your leverage in attracting other entrepreneurs to advertise and sell through your site. The earlier and longer you can hang onto that distinction, the faster your Web site will grow. You'll have top-of-mind share with your first-generation customers. Then you'll benefit from the network effect as first-generation customers tell their friends, who tell their friends, and so on.

The interesting thing about the network effect is this: You must respond to the early surge in attention given to your site by continually supplying visitors with conveniences, services, free content, and so forth. This, in turn, helps draw more visitors and "seller revenue," which will attract even bigger numbers. This is when the network effect kicks in. All visitors reap the benefits from a larger user base. There are more people to interact with in chat rooms and discussion forums; a wider range of products and services to buy; and increased capital for you to spend on upgrading the site with more and better services, tools, and resources. Your growth will model a geometric progression.

RULE 3: DISTINGUISH YOUR BUSINESS FROM OTHERS ONLINE

There are many ways to make your site distinctive, but the best techniques all have one thing in common: They enable customers to do something they can't do through conventional avenues of business. From the customer's perspective, one of the most desirable advantages is greater convenience. Time is increasingly scarce. To do everything we must do and want to do, we crave tools that help us raise our efficiency, save time, and simplify chores.

By its very nature, online shopping takes less time than going to the mall. But the real added value of online shopping is the ease with which shoppers can:

- Get detailed product information that will help them reach a buying decision.

- Conduct product and service comparisons, including price checks.

- Enjoy the benefits of data management systems that enable each customer to establish a personal profile when he or she first enters the site. That profile identifies that person and his or her mailing information and preferences. When customers only need to enter the data once (with the power to update it as needed), they can complete their business more quickly.

- Gain access to customer support 24 hours a day, seven days a week, and 365 days a year through detailed online troubleshooting, FAQs (frequently asked questions) built on a database of the questions most typically asked, and e-mail. The best sites follow through on the promise by making it easy for customers to find the help they need and by responding to e-mail quickly.

- Use tools designed to personalize the shopping experience to the specific needs of each individual and enjoy a more complete shopping experience. For example, e-tailers can position up front the products and services a particular customer orders on a regular basis (such as office supplies or product refills). Make ordering just a click or two away. Also popular are personal address books and online calendars for recording important dates (birthdays, anniversaries, etc.) and alerting customers when it's time to start thinking about shopping or sending a card.

TO GET YOU STARTED, HERE ARE A FEW SOURCES OF VALUE-ADDED TOOLS AND UTILITIES THAT CAN ENHANCE YOUR WEB SITE:

Amazon.com (www.amazon.com/associates), Borders Books (www. search.borders.com/associates/overview.xcv), and Barnes and Noble (www.barnesandnoble.com/affiliate) all offer book sales affiliate programs.

Preview Travel (www.previewtravel.com/Syndication) offers Fare-finder and Travel Newswire services.

OANDA (www.oanda.com/converter/classic) provides currency converters.

Merriam-Webster Online (www.m-w.com) is a dictionary link.

Quote.com (fast.quote.com/fq/products/home) offers financial information products.

The Weather Channel (www.weather.com/aboutus/wxdata.html) provides weather forecasts.

The Sporting News (www.sportingnews.com/logos) links customers to the latest scores.

Website Lunatic (www.biginfo.net/freeserv.html) offers a list of free Web utilities, including polling, messaging, and stock ticker tools.

- Receive e-mails that remind customers of their personal and business schedules (stored in an online calendar that's accessible from anywhere), highlight the arrival of new products that match with the customer's past shopping history, and that include articles and other information that might be of interest to the particular customer.

- Gain access to third-party interactive tools, such as mortgage and retirement calculators; finder services for locating hotels, airline tickets, restaurants, car rentals, and consumer and electronics products at the lowest rates; and books for sale on related topics. To be really innovative, business owners will develop relationships with key vendors who offer services that expand their sites' capabilities. Based on what each business owner has to offer, they might develop a barter arrangement that will result in broader reach and distribution for all parties involved. In some cases, providing access to your site's customer base may be sufficient for you to gain use of a special tool and possibly earn a percentage on each sale initiated through your site.

The way to make your site distinctive is to provide tools and services that go beyond anything typically available offline at a store or through a catalog. The more creative and useful it is, the higher marks your site will receive for distinctiveness.

RULE 4: PUT THE CUSTOMER FIRST

As long as people have been doing business, they have talked about the importance of pleasing the customer. Aside from the good word of mouth you'll enjoy, it is always easier and cheaper to satisfy (and keep) the customers you have than to try to win new business. Experts estimate that the cost of acquiring a new customer costs five to seven times what it takes to retain an existing customer.

In the Internet age, however, the customer truly is king. As a result, companies are striving to provide greater customer service. E-mail gives dissatisfied customers a direct complaint line to the company (often providing access to the highest levels of management). Remember that a customer can abandon even a "killer click" when resolution of a complaint is slow in coming. Never has it been easier for a customer to locate your competition and move on. Above all, many ambitious Web site owners aspire to top-of-mind share among your customers; they are literally fighting over them, offering deeply discounted pricing and distinctive features designed to enhance customers' online experiences. Here are two customer service techniques to consider:

1.   *Be responsive to e-mail.* Even if a final answer will take several days to provide, get back to the customers immediately and tell them when you expect to have an answer.

2.   *Look to new partners and allies to fulfill customer needs.* Amazon.com, for example, has helped revolutionize online partnering by creating relationships with businesses that traditionally would have had nothing in common with the bookselling business. They make it easy for any business to sell books (using Amazon's sales and distribution network). Now, when a customer visits a site that is an Amazon Associate, for example, a health and diet site, that customer can purchase vitamins and exercise equipment, as expected, and can also pick up the latest books on diet and exercise. This added value provides customers with extra convenience and creates a win-win-win situation: Amazon.com effectively expands its online reach, including the prospect of winning a new customer who will come back for more books. Customers enjoy having more of their health and diet needs meet at a single site; they don't have to go to another site to find a book. And the Amazon Associates expand the capabilities of their sites, even earning a small commission on each sale, without having to stock or distribute the books themselves.

RULE 5: DON'T OVERLOOK SIMPLICITY

The KISS, (Keep it Simple, Stupid) factor is critical. It also takes great effort and planning to achieve. A simple site is not necessarily one with only a few pages, limited graphics, and one or two items for sale. Simplicity is a factor of logical navigation and intuitive design that result in a Web site that feels completely natural and appropriate, even to the first-time visitor.

As computer programs have become increasingly robust and rich in features and functions, software developers have faced the challenge of creating interfaces that make using their software intuitive. For many of us, the ultimate test of any software package is our ability to install it and begin using it without opening the manual. The manual should serve as a reference tool rather than as required reading before even opening the software.

True design simplicity is hard to achieve, and most Web sites you visit will fall short. In fact, experiencing a really well-designed site is so extraordinary that when you find one, you'll know it immediately. Everything will appear to be in its logical place; you will navigate the site effortlessly; you will find what you are looking for and perform any transactions quickly and efficiently. One of the rules of design simplicity is to put everything in reach of the customer with no more than two clicks. This is not to say that a greater depth of information should not require more than two clicks; but customers ought to be able to find an overview of their topic within the prescribed two clicks. Expectations of easy access, ease of use, and convenience are so great that customers, with their busy schedules and abbreviated attention spans, will be turned off if your site resembles a game of hide and seek. Always remember that it's easy to use a search engine to find an alternative site (your competition!).

Here are a few of the mistakes business owners and Web site developers make that do more to confuse than simplify customers' online experiences:

- *Making the site search engine hard to spot.* The only possible reason for this error is that business owners are so focused on *what* they are selling that they forget that *where* they are selling it is equally critical. This is analogous to building a supermarket and forgetting to label the aisles, and then making it hard to find an employee who can tell you where the rice is.

- *Trying to be too clever.* It can be fun developing a Web site and coming up with all sorts of interesting and compelling names for the departments and features on your site. Actually, when this is performed carefully and with a lot of thought, subject titles that are slightly out of the ordinary are a plus. They give your visitors a little variety in their online fare. But at all times, the titles you choose should be obvious to the visitor. For example, many sites have a

"What's New" section. If you are tired of this moniker, you might try something more stimulating. If you're a publisher, you might title this section "Hot Off Our Press." This would be perfect if your news was largely devoted to new publications. "Pressing Matters," on the other hand, could be confusing. It's not clear whether it refers to industry news and issues, problems, topics for discussion, or something else entirely.

- *Employing every new technique and technology.* Video, huge graphics, sound, audio, a rainbow of color, and animation don't all have to be used just because they can be done. In most cases, you should not be trying to compete with MTV. By all means, use special effects when they enhance the shopping experience and provide customers with information or convenience. But using technology for technology's sake has never been an acceptable solution, just as using art for art's sake is no way to create a brochure or newsletter. Your goal must always be to help your customers find what they want with the fewest possible distractions and in the shortest amount of time.

RULE 6: ESTABLISH YOUR BRAND

Not all Web sites are designed for e-commerce (online transactions). In fact, the majority of sites are more focused on marketing and brand awareness, although how effectively they accomplish this objective is another matter. Branding can occur at different levels, most typically at the product or service level or at the Web site itself. Manufacturers and distributors will probably be more focused on branding their wares, while a Web site owner or online retailer interested in achieving name recognition will want to focus on branding the Web site itself.

As business owners create more and more relationships online and consolidation eventually begins to focus customers on a smaller set of primary sites, product branding becomes critical. Consider this scenario: In addition to having your own Web site, you want to sell your products on an established cybermall. This particular mall is in great demand because of both the sheer numbers of shoppers who come to the site and the shoppers' upscale demographics. Demand gives top mall owners considerable power, and leveraging that power can make or break a product, particularly a new one. The cybermall owners are in a situation to be highly discriminating, taking only the products they want. They can sell position (and even participation), which is not unlike selling advertising position in a magazine or offering prime shelf space in a supermarket. When a mall or shopping site already has several items in a category, its owners are less likely to feel the need to add your product (regardless of whether it is a new product or you are just late to the online game). On the other hand, strong brand recognition can earn you a mall owner's interest and, possibly, a prominent position on the site.

TIP

Branding can bring shoppers in and educate them. But if you have created the content that can close the sale, why take a chance that a hot prospect will cool? Even if a large number of customers still opt to purchase offline, it may be wise to incorporate into your site the e-commerce capabilities that enable you to close business online, while the shopper is ready to buy. According to a Cyber Dialogue survey of 1,000 small businesses, those that take orders online perform better.

Another reason to focus on building your brand online is that, according to IntelliQuest's IntelliTrack IQ data, there are four times as many shoppers as buyers online today. The higher the price of the item, the more customers are likely to research their purchases online, then buy offline. If your company already enjoys brand awareness and has established products, this will help bring prospective shoppers to your site to check out your latest offerings. But the key to selling customers on your product will be your ability to provide the right information (or content). Doing that and making your online presence known is the essence of Internet branding. Think of your online content as an opportunity to educate your customers. In other words, you are giving them the tools and information to make educated buying decisions. Because no one knows your product or service better than you do, you are the best person to sell it. On your own site, you are not at the mercy of an unknown salesperson, working in a discount store for minimum wage, who may have little or no sales experience or training.

FIGURE 1-1

Benefits and Growth Advantages	Firm Takes Orders Online	Firm Does Not Take Orders Online
Expanded territory	68%	41%
More sales leads	68%	40%
Increased revenue from sales	65%	36%
Stay competitive	54%	47%
Better customer service	47%	52%
Better recruiting	33%	25%
Percentage of total sales from online orders	10%	4%
Online sales have exceeded expectations	12%	2%

Source: Cyber Dialogue.

RULE 7: THE MIDDLEMAN TAKES ON NEW IMPORTANCE

It's been suggested more than once that the Web spells the end of the middleman. It is true that the middleman who merely buys at wholesale and sells at retail may become extinct. Increasingly we find examples of companies selling direct, passing along the savings to their customers. Many a traditional sales force is slowly being replaced by online tools that can help buyers find answers and make many of the decisions they previously left to a sales representative or retailer. Online insurance sales and equity trading are just two examples.

But as the Web continues to grow, adding thousands of new sites and alternatives to your business every day, users become increasingly confused and more lost. The need for a middleman may be stronger than ever. But the online middleman is a new breed, totally reconceived to add real value for Internet users. Internet middlemen—let's call them "e-facilitators"—provide convenience, direction, information, and assistance, all designed to ease the process of finding information, locating a particular Web site, and speeding transactions along. Here are a few examples of the types of sites that serve as Web e-facilitators:

Search engines and directories that help users find the information, companies, and Web sites they want were among the earliest e-facilitators. Many of today's popular portals started as search engines.

Portal or destination sites consolidate many of the essential services and direct links, based on the needs of visitors who match the portal's demographic model.

Cybermalls are online shopping malls that host many companies or products fitting a set of either vertical or horizontal criteria. For example, a mall that appeals to the fashion needs of shoppers might include clothing, footwear, outerwear, sunglasses, jewelry, and accessory stores.

Vertical sites are carefully designed to provide the complete range of services associated with a particular industry. A real estate vertical site might try to think of every service, tool, and product its customers might need. These could include:

- A national database of homes, apartments, and office space available for purchase or lease.

BUILD A VERTICAL BUSINESS

Most stores and businesses are built around a discrete set of products and services. Whether you go to a local clothing retailer, talk with a small manufacturer about producing a new product you have in mind, or make an appointment with your attorney, you can be fairly certain of the range of products and services available. Let's say you are starting up a new business. You need the services of an attorney and an accountant. You'll probably want to have a logo designed. Then you'll need stationery and business cards. You'll have to go to the bank to set up accounts and contact the IRS about getting an Employer Identification Number. You'll need office supplies and furniture, not necessarily available from the same store, and you'll need to purchase or lease computers, telephones, fax machines, and so on. This is the way we are accustomed to shopping for goods and services. Getting it all done takes time and energy away from your real business.

Now imagine a Web site that specializes in small business start-ups. Under one umbrella, you might find all of the above services and equipment. In addition, you could have access to start-up consultants who could help you make the right choices and even assist you in the development of your first business plan. You would only have to out-line your objectives once (albeit in great detail), then the Web-based business would go to work, processing the necessary forms, setting up accounts, and recommending furniture and equipment (based on your specifications). Rather than running all over town, you would make one stop. The convenience such a site could offer is staggering. This is the trend on the Internet. Businesses are providing a wider range of vertical services. You set up one account and have access to a more complete set of tools, services, products, and advice than you can expect from most traditional businesses. Much of this is made possible by business models based on extending relationships. When this new model is carried out successfully, you might just find your Web site elevated to must-see status.

- Background and demographic information about each community, including its schools, churches and temples, shopping, public transportation, local businesses, crime rates, and so on.

- A service that puts prospective buyers in touch with a local real estate agency showing the properties they are interested in seeing. This service could even allow a prospective buyer to make an appointment with an agent online.

- Advice on packing and moving, including checklists of things to do and information about local and national moving companies.

- An online store selling packing and other materials that might help a family prepare for moving day.

- A service designed to help customers put their own homes on the market, including putting them in touch with a local affiliate real estate agency.

- Calculator tools to help customers determine the size of the mortgage they can afford based on current rates. Another useful tool could help customers estimate the price they might get for their old home based on size, age, location, and amenities.

These are just a few ideas to help you start thinking about ways you can use your site to facilitate your customers' online experiences.

RULE 8: BEAT YOUR CUSTOMERS TO THE WEB

In its Spring 1998 "Internet Demographic Study," CommerceNet/Nielsen Media Research reported there were 79 million Internet users in the United States and Canada. When asked how often they use the Internet, 41 million (more than the total number of users just two years before) reported having been online in the past 24 hours. The best news for companies looking at consumer and business-to-business commerce is the fact that 20 million people (fully 25 percent) reported they have purchased online.

At this rate of growth, your customers will be online soon, if they are not already. The United States Internet Council estimates that more than 80 million adults in the United States were online as of January 1999. And a 1998 International Data Corporation report predicted an expansion of Web buyers from 18 million in 1997 to more than 128 million in 2002. What if they come looking for the goods and services you sell, and you're not there? They may find your competitors online instead, and become someone else's customer before you have a chance to win them over.

In an ideal world, you want to enter the market just prior to your customers, which is why you have no time to lose. While I'm not suggesting a mad dash to market, it is time to begin your assessment of the online marketplace in preparation for developing your Web site. Your market analysis should follow four critical steps:

1. Check out the competition.

2. Collect industry and demographic statistics.

3. Create a demographic profile of your ideal customer.

4. Compare your ideal customer with current Web demographics.

With this information, you can make a reasonably accurate determination and will be able to set realistic goals and objectives for your online venture.

Considerable free market research is available online when you know how and where to find it. Start by looking for any competition. Their Web sites will give you insight into how others are approaching your customers. Ask yourself: How are they marketing to prospects? What can I do differently, or better? Are they giving away information, special services, or products? Would I want to buy from them? Do they appear to be succeeding? The last question may be difficult to answer, but you can start by looking for the site counter. This will give you an idea of the number of people who have visited the site.

TIP

Site counters are not completely accurate. First, they may not be set to start at zero. Someone could pad a site counter by starting the count at any number, like 4,000, just to create the illusion of heavier traffic. Also, some counters can't tell you if visitors actually entered the site or spent more than a few seconds looking at the home page. Read site counters with caution and skepticism; you might take an average across several competitive sites.

Industry and Web demographics are somewhat easier to assess. Check out the Web sites of any trade associations, market research and analysis groups, trade journals, or online advertising associations. Some of this information is available for a fee, but if you spend enough time looking through press releases, summaries, and even older reports that have been made public, you can usually find enough information to create an industry snapshot that will serve you well. We'll explore this more in Chapter 2.

Your next task is easier: Develop a detailed profile of your target market. Start by identifying your current customers. Ask yourself if this is the same customer you want to attract online. For example, you might decide to trade up to a bigger, richer customer; or you may want to broaden the market for your products and services to include both large and small customers. Whatever the case, learn as much as you can about your customers: what they buy from you, how much they spend on an average order, what else they buy online, and where they tend to shop. The more you know the better.

The final step is to compare your ideal customer profile with the demographics of the current online population. You may find that your customers are already online, just waiting for a business like yours to serve them. If this is the case, you need to act quickly. Get your site up and make your presence known. Put your Web address on your brochures, catalogs, business cards, and stationery—every piece of paper that leaves your office. Register with the major search engines and directories. You'll also need to integrate your Web site into your total marketing strategy. This is the most often underestimated and ignored advice. I can't overemphasize the importance of marketing your Web site and the products and services you offer, and keeping those efforts in line with and tied to your general business planning. I've seen companies use one theme or tagline in their print advertising and promote an entirely different message online, thus watering down the effectiveness of their marketing in both mediums.

If you are rushing to bring your business online, remember that you don't have to resolve every issue and provide a full range of services your first day online. Sites are dynamic; they can grow over time. Even if you only hint at the services to come in the weeks and months ahead (if possible, give customers a timetable for their delivery), you have a better chance of stemming attrition. If you remain true to your promises and deliver on time, customers who are satisfied with the quality of your products and services will continue to return.

One word of advice: If you currently have a printed catalog or are known to carry a very extensive product line, don't try to limit your initial online offering to a small subset of your products. This is not the way to test the viability of e-commerce. In fact, you stand a good chance of frustrating current customers who know you have much more to offer. When you feel you are ready to support e-commerce, roll out your offerings in their entirety. Better still, provide even more choice online in an effort to encourage customers to use your Web site. Keep your message consistent and on target and broadcast it loud and clear. We'll look at marketing techniques in greater detail in Chapters 8 and 9.

As companies expand their online capabilities, development typically follows a pattern: The first step is to gain companywide access to the Internet. This helps build familiarity and facilitates the use of online research. Second, businesses begin to provide some means for communicating with customers, either through e-mail or with a small Web site that delivers marketing and branding information as well as a direct link to the company's e-mail. The third stage is e-commerce, which enables customers to order or shop for products and services online. This requires advertising and promotion of the site and, eventually, support for online transactions. Finally, as business owners and staff begin to appreciate the full capabilities of the Internet, they turn to e-business. By this stage, they are taking advantage of administrative tools, online human resource support, new employee recruitment, internal communications, schedule management, and automatic inventory management.

The key to success is to be prepared for the business to come. Be there to greet your customers when they come browsing or shopping; provide the features and functions that will help create an instant bond; respond to their needs; engage them in an ongoing dialogue; and build a thriving and long-term relationship. Sometimes you can become one of your customers' favorite sites just by being there, open for business, when they come calling.

TIP

If you have inventory (including older parts and models) that you feel are not cost-effective to market in your print catalog or through direct mail, your Web sit may be the ideal venue. It won't cost much more to include these items, and you can discount the prices in the hope of moving out some of this older inventory.

RULE 9: ONE TIME IS NOT ENOUGH

The secret to any successful business is a customer base of satisfied shoppers and loyal buyers who keep coming back for more. Not only will this help to sell your goods and services; it will give you the kind of visitation statistics that prospective online advertisers love. You will also find it easier to build relationships with other companies and put together joint ventures when you have something they want: loyal customers.

WHAT IS E-BUSINESS?

In simplest terms, e-business is everything you do online. E-commerce (marketing, branding, and sales transactions) is actually a subset of e-business. E-business encompasses all the resources and services you develop for customers, employees, suppliers, indeed everyone with whom you do business. Having an online employee manual is an example of doing e-business. So is an online system that automates reordering of supplies from key vendors. If you rely on a field force, give these men and women the tools to sell more effectively and close business on the spot. For example, give them online access to current inventory data and tools that can help them calculate the price of an order, apply any discounts, and set delivery dates. Similarly, your customers will appreciate tools that enable them to track their orders, check shipping dates, and solve problems online.

As you build your Web site, you face two simultaneous challenges: 1) to reach new prospects and 2) to build customer loyalty. Marketing and branding can help with the first challenge. The second requires the right products, an easy-to-use Web site, and exemplary customer service. IDC reports that 92 percent of online merchants have programs designed to build loyalty through some combination of customer service, personalization, mass customization, and personalized content.

While there are many technical tricks and graphical theatrics that suggest personalization (such as greeting repeat visitors by name), true personalization and customization require sophisticated programming and database management. If you can afford it, it's worth the cost and effort. But don't overlook two straightforward, relatively simple strategies: Be responsive to customer requests and reply to e-mail quickly. Show you care.

Another important way to keep customers coming back is by creating the expectation of finding something new each time they visit. Your Web site should have a shorter shelf life than your print brochure or catalog. Keep it fresh. This doesn't mean you need to redesign your Web site every month, but it does require you to add new content, and the more often the better. Some Web site owners recommend adding something every day. If you can't handle that kind of schedule or are at a loss as to what to add every day, try a weekly update schedule. At the very least, provide monthly additions. Post the current date on your Web site to indicate a dynamic site that is kept current. Some sites actually post the time of day, suggesting that their Web sites are up-to-the-minute.

One way to help you manage frequent changes and additions is to create elements on your site that lend themselves to easy update:

- *Success stories* (as you build up an archive of stories, classify them by product or industry).

- *Headlines* (you can swap these daily and even use them to promote a particular product, service, or special offer).

- *Special offers* (even a small discount is news).

- *Press releases* (even if you don't send them out to the news services or trade journals, you can write online releases for visitors to read).

- *Company and customer news* (broadcast company hires, promote new suppliers and any special relationships, and list key new accounts).

- *Interactive tools* (while you won't have to update these as often, you can add a new one every few months, and a truly useful tool will encourage customers to return regularly).

- *Discussion forums* (enable your customers and visitors to exchange thoughts on topics pertinent to your business or industry. This one takes some of the pressure off of you and your staff to develop content).

- *Monthly e-letters* (online newsletters sent to customers' and visitors' e-mail accounts inform them about special offers, new products, new features on the site and remind them to come back and see what's new).

THE SECRET TO "STICK"

In the language of the Web, having repeat visitors and loyal customers is called "stick." How often these people return determines your degree of "stickiness." And believe me, you want stick. All 11 of these critical rules are designed to help you achieve stick. But to simplify the secret to stick and distill it down to one phrase: Provide value. Whether through your pricing, convenience, ease of use, customer service, information, or tools, your objective is to create a Web site that provides customers with value. When you are trying to evaluate your own site, or that of a competitor, look for the value.

To help you measure the relative value of sites, try creating a scale from 0 to 10, with 0 being no value and 10 being exceptional value. By defining each value in your scale, you can begin to develop a methodology for assessing Web sites. For example, 1 might identify sites with limited product information, poor organization, and no e-commerce capabilities. If you follow through with this exercise and use it when analyzing your competition, you will develop a skilled eye and better insight into what works online.

RULE 10: TAKE FULL ADVANTAGE OF THE INTERNET

The Internet is a new medium. It combines the technology of television, computers, telephone, cable, printing, radio, and more to create the most powerful communication medium ever experienced. As the Internet continues to mature, the distinctions between the many technologies become less obvious. In short, the Internet is melding these technologies into a new, holistic medium. However, in thinking about your Web site, don't overlook the power of each technology.

For example, it is faster, easier, and less expensive to develop and distribute material online than to write, design, print, and mail traditional catalogs and brochures. For this reason, do not hesitate to schedule the introduction of new products and services. In fact, you should put them up on your site immediately. Mala Gunadasa-Rohling, a Web designer and owner of eSeeds (www.eseeds.com), an e-commerce site dedicated to the needs of horticulturists, estimates she adds roughly 200 new products to eSeeds every week.

The cost to add the text and graphics is minimal, and anything new not only brings freshness to your site, but gives you something else to market and sell. Don't think in terms of your print catalog or brochure when managing your Web site. Even when you don't have new products to list, change your images and photos regularly and add more information to existing categories. Perhaps you could have a whole series of product shots taken at one time, showing the product being used in different situations, environments, and industries. Swapping these in and out (or writing a program that shows customers a different image each time they visit) can give products a much wider appeal. What sparks the interest of one prospective buyer may do nothing for another. "Our customers appreciate the breadth of detail we provide on every book and every plant we sell," explains Gunadasa-Rohling. "But it takes time to add that depth of detail. So while we add 200 products a week, we continue filling in the detail on existing offerings over a longer period of time."

Hyperlinks and hot links are also unique to this environment. Thanks to the power of the computer, these tools enable you to add more information in an orderly and logical format. You provide the links; your customers decide how much they want to see. By linking to other Web sites you think your visitors would appreciate, you add another dimension to the richness and added value you are able to provide. The very act of linking to another site gives you some leverage in gaining a reciprocal link on that site. A reciprocal link increases your chances of being found by a prospective customer who is predisposed to want what you have to sell.

The computer also enables you to make your site interactive, something you can't do nearly as effectively in print. While you can include questionnaires and worksheets in a brochure, it's not the same as working online. Responses are automatically tabulated in real time, and the answers can be more personalized and presented in greater depth. Some interactive tools serve as a way for customers to prepare a series of "what if" scenarios that will help them reach the critical decision to buy. Interactive tools also make it easier to provide customers with personalized information, which everyone appreciates.

Create e-letters (electronic newsletters) and send them to your customers' e-mail accounts. In fact, it doesn't cost any more to send them to everyone who asks to be on your recipient list. In addition to being a very cost-effective way to communicate with customers on a regular basis, e-letters can contain hyperlinks to bring customers and prospects directly to your site quickly and effortlessly. When they read something they like or want to know more about, all they do is click on the hypertext address you provide, and the appropriate page in your Web site appears automatically.

Offer your e-letter free of charge to anyone who fills out a request form. You can use the form to collect customer information, which will help you build a demographic profile of customers. To maintain customers' privacy, separate customer information from names and mailing addresses and treat the information anonymously to build a collective impression of the "typical" customer. Explain what you are doing to ease customer concerns. This assurance, along with the inducement of receiving a free e-letter, will encourage more people to join your mailing list. You can use this information in several ways: 1) to put customers on a mailing list to receive your e-letters; 2) to personalize visitors' Web site experience; and 3) to tailor content, services, and product offerings to the greatest majority of customers. Some sites are designed to track each customer's online reading and buying habits. With this information, the site owner can send personalized e-mails alerting each customer of new shipments and services they are most likely to want.

TIP

When creating an e-letter that references information and products available on your Web site, embed a hypertext link that takes the reader directly to the relevant page...not to your home page.

LOSE YOUR OLD MODELS, BUT USE YOUR ADVANTAGES

"People experienced in media businesses who want to re-purpose some of their content for the Web have also been in the business of selling advertising before; they appreciate its value," says Tim Koogle, Yahoo!'s chairman and CEO. "When their business is well run, they can do incremental business online that builds on the economies of scale achieved. If managed well, theoretically the incremental cost for reusing content you have already authored or paid for is small. It's important for those who have been in existing media businesses, whether broadcast or print, to realize that their traditional model for doing business does not directly translate to the Web and can hurt their ability to fully leverage the Web. This spells opportunities for start-ups."

Koogle continues: "But start-ups face a problem of their own, which has to do with the cost of generating original content and distributing it only on the Internet. They must hire the creative people—writers, artists, and so forth. And the creative people have to carefully match the focus of the business. They may need to be local or spread around the world. Whatever the case, success depends on one's ability to manage the business closely, keep a lid on costs, be realistic about assets, and not let expenses get ahead of the curve."

RULE 11: INTEGRATE YOUR OFFLINE BUSINESS AND YOUR E-BUSINESS

Above all, remember that an effective Web site does not exist in a vacuum. It must be an integral part of your business. Failing to completely integrate the Web into every facet of business and marketing decision making may be the most common mistake that traditional companies make. It may be easier to think in terms of the holistic picture when your business is exclusively on the Internet, but that doesn't lessen the need for integration. Even an online business must make marketing and business decisions that involve traditional avenues of promotion and advertising.

Every decision must be made with implications for your Web site as part of the mix. Just as all your print materials must include your Web site address, so budget allocations should include ongoing Web site development, marketing efforts, and e-business applications.

At an even more basic level, you need to factor the Internet into your general business thinking and planning. For example, ask yourself whether there are processes that could be performed more efficiently and cost-effectively online. Challenge each traditional assumption. On the Internet, you potentially have the power to solve supply chain problems, save money, decrease time to market, and turn traditional cost centers into profit centers. This is at the heart of what we refer to as e-business. For example, when Federal Express' management decided to put package tracking online, they revolutionized customer service. More importantly, they freed customer service representatives from a constant and growing barrage of telephone calls, thus enabling more employees to focus on new customer services.

Do the math, calculate the time saved, assess the pros and cons of moving applications online, and build a business plan that includes the Web. This is the basis for doing e-business. In your Web site you have a powerful tool. You're not enjoying your maximum advantage if you continue to treat it as an afterthought.

By observing and practicing these eleven rules, you will be on your way to getting the most out of your investment in a Web site. The tools and expert advice in the chapters that follow will equip you to put these critical steps into action. You'll see how experienced business owners and Web site developers apply them in everything they do.

TURN RELATIONSHIPS INTO COMMUNITIES

F ollowing the development of the Internet continues to be much more than an exercise in keeping up with the dramatic development of technology. It requires an understanding of people: how they communicate, what they need (and want) to know, and, with the more recent expansion of e-commerce and e-business, what and how they purchase.

Because our lives revolve around the need to build relationships, both personal and professional, the Internet's capacity for communication should be exploited as a tool for any business venture. In the space of about four years, mass online participation has developed from personal expression (through e-mail and personal home pages) to an arena that includes business models and social interrelationships unlike anything we have ever experienced. Given the Web's capacity to support communications—the backbone of relationship building—we can expect to witness a continuing evolution in the years to come.

THE EVOLUTION OF MASS COMMUNICATION

Let's look back in time for a moment in order to better understand the significance of technology's impact on communication. I have identified three
watershed inventions that, in my opinion, have changed the course of public communication. I have chosen them not so much for their technological
innovation—although they all represent breakthroughs in technology—but
for their contribution to the way we communicate and their ability to put the
power of communications in the hands of a broader base of people. In other
words, each invention has helped to open wider the doors of communication for every man, woman, and child. With each step forward, we have
found it easier and more cost-effective to share thoughts, opinions and, yes,
marketing messages with the world.

The communications revolution began in 1455 with the introduction of
the Gutenberg printed Bible. When Johannes Gutenberg demonstrated the
potential of his printing press, the public was quick to respond. For the first
time, printed material could be produced in quantities large enough to dis-
seminate beyond the nobility and the clergy. The instant reception of both
the product and the process is evidenced by the fact that within only 50
years of the debut of the printing press, the city of Milan had more than 300
printers. Over the years, we have continued to enjoy and learn from the
fruits of printers' labors.

New forms of expression developed. In addition to books, we came to
read posters, handbills, newspapers, magazines, and more to keep up on the
social, political, and business news of the day. Reading grew from a skill
reserved for the very wealthy and professionals (e.g., clergy, physicians,
and attorneys) to a basic requirement of living. Through the centuries, illit-
eracy has become the exception, not the rule.

We travel forward now to the 1980s, when we were introduced to desktop publishing. With a computer, a printer, and word processing and desktop design software, we started to create and print our own newsletters,
flyers, brochures, magazines, and books—with or without the aid of pro-

fessional printers. Without debating the quality of the design that goes into much of this homegrown work, we can agree that the floodgates of communication burst open. Companies that previously felt they could not afford to hire outside communications help suddenly had the means to express themselves.

Then came the Internet, quite probably the greatest contribution to the communications revolution. It gives every computer the potential to serve as a printing press, broadcast system, and place of assembly. Most important, the Internet has opened the door to two-way communication. In fact, it's the capacity for two-way communication that causes me to discount several significant technological breakthroughs, like telegraph, radio, and television. So you ask, Where does that leave the telephone? It's certainly an example of two-way communication, but its reach is limited primarily to real-time discussion with the person at the other end. Even if we factor in voice mail and conference calls, its impact on mass communication is not nearly as dramatic as that of desktop publishing or the Internet. These inventions did more than expand the breadth and speed of communications; they put greater and greater potential power over communication into the hands of the individual.

When we combine our basic need for relationships with the Internet's great capacity for communication, we can understand the rapid growth and evolution of the online phenomenon of communities. When taken out of this larger context, many will argue that the popularity of online communities is only a passing fad. As technology advances, these critics will probably be proven correct. It's always possible (actually probable) that some new technology will eventually supplant the Internet. But as a means to accomplishing the goals of both business and society to build and strengthen relationships through the power of communication, the Internet today is the best tool we have and will remain the logical precursor of everything yet to come. Our challenge is take advantage of this technology's capacity to help us personalize or humanize information and communications. We identify with communities and portals and look to them to provide the tools and venues to reach our audiences.

BUILDING ONLINE RELATIONSHIPS

Possibly the most eloquent description of the potential of the online community comes from Howard Rheingold, a friend, prolific author, speaker, and longtime advocate of the computer's power to expand—rather than reduce—human contact and relationships. During a recent interview, he described his own experiences online:

"I ended up dancing at three weddings of people who I met in my virtual community. I went to three funerals as well. I spoke at two of those funerals. I sat with two people as they were dying, people I would not have known, and who would not have known me otherwise.... In the happy times of my life, I've celebrated with these people. I've entrusted my daughter to them as baby-sitters. I've stayed with them in their homes in Tokyo, Paris, New York, Vancouver, and Sidney, Australia...all over the world. You can't tell me that you can't find a community online. And you can't tell the parents of a son who's been suffering from leukemia for a number of years, who have had an online support group to help them through those hard times...it does exist."

You don't have to look far on the World Wide Web to find examples of what Howard is talking about. A parent develops Alzheimer's Disease, and the children want to know what they can do to help improve her quality of life. They go to the Web and search on Alzheimer's Disease, where they find more than 35,000 sites. Among them is www.alz.org, which includes information on treatment, research, care, support networks, and much more.

Pet owners have been using the Web as both a source of information and a community for sharing stories of loved animals. The Virtual Pet Cemetery (www.lavamind.com/pet.html) is a place to immortalize a favorite pet through pictures and the sharing of stories of love and devotion. While therapeutic for the grieving pet owners, visiting the Virtual Pet Cemetery can be a heart-wrenching experience for any animal lover. In addition to this site, the Web abounds with sources for purchasing pet toys and food, learning about animal breeders, and receiving veterinary advice—both canned (in the form of articles and lists of frequently asked questions, or FAQs) and as responses to a pet owner's specific query.

Parents represent another group that benefits from a rich cache of online resources that provide advice, discussions, resources, education, and activities for parents and their children. Parent Soup (www.parentsoup.com) is perhaps the best-known site in this category. Within the community of parents, many sites are developing to serve specific subsets of parents and their unique needs and demographics. Single parents, for example, can share experiences with other single parents, find parenting advice, and learn about special programs for their children. The site Daddy's Home (www.daddyshome.com) gives fathers who serve as the primary caregivers to their children recipes to cook, activities, advice, and the opportunity to share experiences and discuss children with other fathers. Similarly, there are several sites designed to cater to the needs of working mothers.

These sites are largely free to users. The intent of their developers is to create communities built around very specific personal and financial demographics (such as kids, Generation X, baby boomers, or seniors) or around a particular need or activity (health care, pets, career, dating, etc.). The fact that many of these services are provided free of charge has been a source of controversy. Critics have questioned the ability of these sites to survive, given the fact that hosting a Web site does have its associated costs, in both dollars and time. The critics are right, insofar as many of these sites do disappear after a matter of months; but they are also wrong.

When Web site developers or owners set out with a thoughtful concept, a well-conceived plan, and enough funding (critical), their sites can grow and succeed. Advertising is one source of revenue, although it can be harder to secure than many site owners realize. In keeping with the earlier discussion about the Internet creating new models for business, a Web site that doesn't sell anything but is able to capture the interest of a large base of Web users and keep them coming back for more can be of real interest and value to other business owners. This value is the source of many of the acquisitions and mergers we hear so much about these days. When a commercial venture buys one of these sites, it is really buying a prospective customer base, not a Web site per se.

"In our case, our e-commerce site (eSeeds) developed out of our experience with the horticultural community online," explains Mala Gunadasa-Rohling. "I began developing Web sites for Canadian garden clubs in late 1995 and early 1996. As this community continued to grow online and we found ourselves answering more and more questions about where to purchase various items, we realized this was an opportunity we should grasp." Furthermore, Gunadasa-Rohling's business is testimony to the ability of community and e-commerce to thrive side by side. She continues to develop Web sites for the ever-increasing horticultural community online. To date, Gunadasa-Rohling estimates her business Tapestry International has developed and maintains sites for 45 garden clubs, two botanical gardens, the CBC Canadian Gardener, and several other groups. At the same time, she continues to build and maintain eSeeds and receives more and more business every month from the online community.

HOWARD RHEINGOLD ON COMMUNITY

While there are any number of basic tenets of good Web design, virtually everyone you talk with will have his or her own perspective about what constitutes the critical component. In the interview that follows, Howard Rheingold focuses on the significance of building a community around your Web site.

> RHEINGOLD: *The fact that you communicate with computers doesn't mean that you have a community. But people affect each other's lives by the thousands every day.*
>
> *The online community is something that's been gaining momentum for some time. For more than a decade, people have been reaching out to each other through electronic bulletin boards, online conferencing, Usenet news groups, mailing lists, e-mail, MUDs [multiuser domains], chat rooms, and IRC [Internet Relay Chat] channels. Scholarly, scien-*

tific, political, and community knowledge is being exchanged in a way that's never been possible before.

This is the first medium in which many people have had access to many other people—through articles, quick postings, chat and discussion groups, and e-mail. And at the same time the Web promotes many-to-many communications, it also enables one person at a time to speak up. In other words, even though it's many-to-many, it's not broadcast. It can be, but it doesn't have to be. Electric Minds, the site I created in the spring of 1996, grew out of that vision. I saw the Web come along and create this wonderful visual control panel for the Internet, the way the graphical user interface created a visual control panel for personal computers. This visual environment produces an ease of use and an unimposing look that is bringing all kinds of people onto the Internet.

The Web is a wonderful multimedia publishing medium that anyone can use to publish inexpensively to the world. But it ought to be more; it ought to be a social communication medium. My mission was twofold: to show that people could use the Web to communicate with each other on a many-to-many basis, and to raise and broaden discourse about technology. Electric Minds is a community on the Web (www.minds.com) where all kinds of people—kids, old folks, homemakers, you name it— can talk about technology and the way it affects their lives.

Between November 1996 and March 1997, we grew to about 50,000 subscribers, people who have signed up at least once. Time magazine named us one of the ten best Web sites of the year.

Minds.com was our flagship, our prototype, our farm team, and our demonstration proof of concept. The next phase is using our expertise to help others create communities around other topics—both within organizations and out in the consumer space—for companies that want to build a new kind of relationship with their vendor community, developers, and customers.

We are a combination of a consulting firm and a talent agency. We help people in organizations think through what their goals are, who their audience is, who their customers are, and what their social contract with those people should be. Then we help them make decisions about the kinds of resources they're willing to invest toward achieving their goals.

A few people are beginning to discover that a virtual community doesn't just happen. You don't just throw up a discussion forum on your Web site and expect intelligent conversation to happen there. It must be carefully planned, grown, maintained, and nurtured. We hire, train, and manage the people who do the support, the coaching, the online facilitation, the hosting, the knowledge sharing, and the editing. All these steps are required to digest the basic information into a form others can use, whether that's creating a forum useful in a single-business, business-to-business, or business-to-community context. All the while, the goal for minds.com remains to keep an open forum for just about anyone who wants to talk about technology.

AUTHOR: *In terms of this being applicable to businesses, I want to throw out an idea and get your reaction. When mail-order giant Spiegel first went online, it did something that I feel was amazing, and actually ahead of its time. It was not so much an e-commerce site as an e-business site. You could purchase a few items found in the catalog, but, more importantly, you were introduced to the people behind the business. Here was a business everyone knew, and yet didn't really know at all. The catalog and the 800 number kept it very remote and impersonal. You didn't know the buyers at all, and the customer service people were anonymous individuals you called only when necessary.*

So suddenly Spiegel goes online and introduces customers and prospects to its staff. We were given their names and shown pictures of the departmental buyers, marketers, and even technical staff. We were invited to contact them and engage in conversation. For example, you might be interested in table linens and want to know about stemware and cutlery that would look particularly nice with your choice in tablecloth and napkins. It was easy to send off an e-mail note to the buyer in housewares and ask for an opinion. It seems ironic that this so-called impersonal device called a computer actually put shoppers in touch with people who had remained invisible for decades.

That format didn't last very long. I'm sure management felt it was too unsophisticated and touchy-feely, but I think it stands as an excellent example of what you are describing: bringing the community concept to business.

RHEINGOLD: *Absolutely. Establishing relationships is what business is really about. And here we have a great tool for creating relationships on an ongoing basis. Amazon.com is a perfect example. In a site both rich in content and sophisticated in message, Amazon.com's Jeff Bezos has created a community of people talking about books. It's not just a place to order books; it's a place to talk about books. That's true of many other sites as well. Creating communities of interest can be good business.*

AUTHOR: *What does it take for a business to move in the direction of community and build the forums, content, and support structure it needs to survive?*

RHEINGOLD: *First of all, you need someone who knows how this medium works. Don't expect to become an expert overnight. That's what we're in the business to do.*

You may have people in-house who spend a lot of time online. Take advantage of their experience. That's the best advice I could give you.

Because Electric Minds was an early player in the community arena, the impact of what Rheingold and his staff were doing may have been lost on many businesses. That has subsequently changed, and increasingly business owners have begun to think of their sites as communities for their industry, profession, product line, and so on. After an enviably strong start, Rheingold sold Electric Minds to Santa Barbara-based Durand Communications Inc. in July 1997. In addition to maintaining Electric Minds, Durand develops and markets CommunityWare, an interactive Web site service that hosts both free public communities and private communities (for a monthly fee). One of the advantages of CommunityWare is that it does not require customers to download special software or a proprietary browser. At the time of the acquisition, Electric Minds had grown to 80,000 members, all of whom became prospective customers for Durand's services.

Rheingold is still pursing his objectives to provide professional consulting services to businesses interested in creating communities. In 1999, he opened a new, private Web-conferencing community. The Brainstorms

Community (www.rheingold.com/community.html) can be accessed by invitation or approval only.

CULTIVATING A BUSINESS COMMUNITY

There is some controversy over the value of applying the concept of community to commercial and business-to-business sites. In particular, the dissidents argue that we should be running businesses, not hosting gathering spots. Businesspeople, they maintain, do not run their businesses as communities. Why should their Web sites be run that way?

I respond to this line of thinking with a simple reminder: The Web is different. Its roots are different. Until very recently, neither the Internet nor the World Wide Web was considered a viable medium for commercial transactions. Remember, the Internet began as a communication system used primarily by scientists, government employees, and educators. They weren't trying to sell anything, except maybe the acceptance of their ideas. The Internet was a great big network of information and resources. It was never intended to be a giant shopping mall in cyberspace.

That was then. Today businesses of all sizes are charging onto the Web, each trying to outdo the competition. Even so, the old roots are strong and have been slow to change. Among longtime Internet users, there still lurks some resentment concerning the Internet's recent commercialism. This is one reason why most unsolicited, online broadcast e-mailings (electronic direct mail) or spams are not well received. Traditionalists expected the Internet to remain primarily a resource for free information. They predicted that even commercial sites would give away more than they sold, even if it was only information.

That has not been the case. The Web has very quickly become a commercial entity. This may be largely due to the increase in new users during the past two years. Millions of new Netizens have no history or preconceived notion regarding the Web. They are inundated with television advertising invading their living rooms, direct mail filling their mailboxes, and infomercials urging them to shop when they should be sleeping. Why should the Internet be any different? If anything, they are pleasantly surprised at the amount of high-quality content they can receive and use for free.

As the Internet continues to grow, more and more businesses will come to appreciate the need for and value of communities. To prove my point, try typing in a subject on any of the major search engines. If you receive any fewer than 9,000 responses, I'll be surprised. With so much information (and misinformation) to wade through, companies have to make a special effort to stand out from the crowd and attract loyal users and customers. For consumers, selecting a site on the Web is like going shopping in a mall with 20,000 pet stores or 100,000 clothing outlets. How do you choose? You choose by picking the ones that:

- *Come up first in a Web search,* a position extremely difficult to maintain for long;

- *Have well-recognized brand names,* like Staples, IBM, BMW, or F.A.O. Schwarz;

- *Do everything possible to promote and advertise* their Web sites, online and through more traditional media such as radio and print; or

- *Are recognized for providing a wealth of additional information,* including links to related Web sites, online discussions, professional advice, and news—what we call added value.

The last criterion is what commercial community Web sites are all about. Thinking of your site as a community helps you focus on your customer demographics—who is most likely to buy. Once you know this, it is easier to invent the tools, services, and information that will provide the greatest value. This may sound a little like becoming a portal, but there is an important difference: The owners of commercial communities are interested in attracting customers who need to buy something. It's a way to beat out the competition and gain top-of-mind market share. Portals strive to become the first site users log onto each session, and the site they return to throughout a session. In short, a portal is one's personal gateway to the

Internet and home base for gaining access to services ranging from e-mail and search engines to personalized information and Web-site development and hosting.

As for the critics' belief that traditional businesses do not rely on community, consider that Barnes and Noble, Borders, and a number of other bookstores are striving to create a sense of community in their brick-and-mortar stores when they open coffee bars. Suddenly this is no longer just a bookstore, but a place where you gather with other book lovers. You're encouraged to browse and sip a cup of coffee while you flip through your books and magazines. To add to the atmosphere, many of the same bookstores also hold book signings, monthly lectures, and discussions related to a current best-seller or literary topic. All of this goes to create a congenial atmosphere that encourages people to buy and return regularly. In short, community helps build loyalty. No one would think of accusing these booksellers of going soft by inviting people to come in and hang out in the store. They want to sell books, and they have hit upon a way to create an environment that helps achieve that goal.

We tell clients that selling is more than creating hype and putting a price tag on a product or service. Given the degree of sophistication among customers today, you need to give them the means to make an informed decision. In other words, you need to educate your customers and prospects and, at the same time, encourage them to look to you as the ultimate source of that knowledge…and the related products and services.

In a sense, this is what a commercial Web site community does. It builds credibility for you as a knowledgeable resource. If people believe you are an expert with a lot to offer, it's not such a leap for them to believe that your products and services are superior. Besides, buying from you is their way of repaying you for your guidance and assistance. They are showing their loyalty to you. A community Web site helps create an environment that provides customers and prospects with value-added advice and education and, in turn, builds loyalty.

Communities also help generate the network effect. Quite simply, the premise is that the more people participate in the activities of a particular

Web site (subscribe to its offerings, fill out customer profiles, or shop), the greater the benefit for all. For example, more people will be available to share their thoughts about your products and the industry in general. This is an excellent way to generate word-of-mouth support. Furthermore, if your site is well visited, you will have a better chance of gaining additional revenue from advertising and joint ventures. Everyone wants to partner with a winner, and a large customer base helps distinguish you as exceptional. This added revenue and the promotion of special joint ventures allows you to pass added benefits on to your customers, in the form of more content and services and a broader base of commercial offerings. This, in turn, helps bring additional visitors, prospects, and customers. The result is a classic cyclical growth spiral.

Finally, there's the matter of entertainment. Given that most computer monitors bear a very close resemblance to a television screen and some commercial Web sites try to outdo MTV in giving their visitors a multimedia experience, it's not surprising that many people think of the Web as an alternative form of entertainment. In fact, surveys suggest that television has been one of the primary victims of the Internet. Increasingly, people are spending their spare time "surfing the Net" rather than "vegging out" in front of the tube. A Lexmark-sponsored report in 1998 found that among online users:

- 57 percent would rather give up their televisions than their computers.

- 66 percent would part with their stereos before their computers.

- 55 percent would even give up the convenience of their automatic dishwashers before parting with their computers.

As business owners, then, your challenge is to apply the concept of community to your online business, either business-to-consumer or business-to-business. Every business needs customers, whether consumers or other business buyers. This is a need that traditional brick-and-mortar businesses and online businesses share. For both, the challenge is to get shoppers into the store and convert them into buyers. An offline business may use print, television, and radio advertising, special promotions, public relations, loss leaders, brand marketing, cache, location, and environment to attract prospects. The online business does much the same. To a large extent the difference resides in the medium, not in the strategy or tactics.

One technique, however, is unique to the Web, and is certainly less expensive to develop. Quite simply, if you make your site *the source* for information, ideas, products, resources, and more, your site has the potential to become *the place* people think of first when they want to buy, discuss, or learn about anything related to your industry or service. Here's how it works: Start by identifying the demographic profile you wish to make the basis of your online community. Who are you trying to reach? What is your message? What is your objective once you reach them?

Next, build a set of tools, services, products, links, and other activities that will keep your ideal audience coming back for more and, more importantly, coming to you *first*. You want to build a site that so effectively services the requirements of your audience that they associate your business and your Web site with their first line of contact. In other words, they attribute to you the ability to fill their immediate needs in most cases. If you can't provide the specific service or product they require, at least you can help them find it. Your capacity to provide important links to related sites, build relationships with other vendors, and attract appropriate advertising to your site plays an important role here.

If you want to appeal to business buyers, you should further strive to position yourself as a vertical community. Once you set your objectives, begin forging relationships within your industry that enable you to be the full-service vendor. In some cases, you might function more as an Internet Transaction Broker, passing the business directly through to the company with whom you have a relationship and keeping a small percentage of the revenue for your service. Sometimes the company with which you affiliate will have content (a tool, service, even helpful articles) you can integrate directly into your site. Your site will be the richer for the content, your customers will discover a site that lives up to their expectations, and you will be forging the kinds of relationships that function best in the new economy the Web is generating.

Once you begin to build such relationships, remember that the process never ends. You need to constantly enrich your site by adding new tools, new functionality, and new ways for customers to share their experiences and expertise. When it comes to word of mouth, the Web is not very different from traditional business; it just facilitates the process by providing online forums for interaction and the exchange of information. Amazon.com, for example, invites readers to express their views about every book, CD, and video it sells.

Further validation for communities comes from a development that the critics probably never imagined: the increasing number of private sites. In some cases, the privacy is used to require prospective customers to gain access by parting with personal information, which will enable the Web sites' owners to better profile their customer base. In other cases, business owners want to charge users an access fee to select information and services. Still others want to limit access to information they consider private. Intranets and extranets fall into this last category. When management wants to limit data access to only their employees (information such as human resources information, selling strategies, or inventory information), they create a private Web site for internal use only, called an intranet. Similarly, companies have data that is only for other companies in their business circle, such as their subsidiaries, suppliers, developers, value-added resellers, and joint venture partners. These outside companies can gain access to the extranet, but only with authorization. All of these entities are types of communities.

There is one more category of community that experts believe will become increasingly popular in the months and years ahead. These are private trade communities, which are similar to extranets except that they enable all authorized participants to do business with one another in a sort of private buying consortium or cooperative. The objective in designing and maintaining a private business-to-business trade community is to create an environment that facilitates trade by providing direct and easy access to one another, enabling members to post and read articles and to share tools and links of interest to the specific group. Keeping it private helps the site owner control its size and manageability. These sites perform both e-commerce and e-business tasks, but their main function is to create convenience through a closely managed community. As Web sites become increasingly ubiquitous and a standard component to doing business, their focus is expected to narrow. Site owners will cut away the chaff and focus on the kernels of information and the services most beneficial to the target audience.

A SITE FOR BOOK LOVERS

Perhaps one of the best-known examples of business as community is Amazon.com, both for the quality of the site and the fact that its developers first implemented many of the techniques we take for granted today. This is not just a large online bookstore; it is a community of book lovers (and more recently music and video lovers as well). It offers visitors sample chapters of best-selling new books, interviews with authors, and many reviews, both professional reviews and those written by other Amazon.com visitors. All this helps build the online community.

Amazon.com is a successful commercial site. In addition to all the extras it offers visitors, Amazon.com makes ordering quick and easy. The navigation is logical and the search engine powerful. In addition, the system monitors your preferences and buying habits, then responds by showing you similar books in like categories. With your permission, Amazon.com will even notify you via e-mail when new books in your favorite category arrive. By registering yourself and your credit card information, you can take advantage of one-click shopping. Customers are protected by a secure system for handling credit transactions.

Perhaps the most inventive aspect of Amazon.com is the Associates program, a model for distribution that is becoming a standard among commercial sites. The Associates program allows Amazon.com to leverage its distribution network by reaching out to the communities growing on other sites. Rather than limit sales to customers who come to the site through advertising and word of mouth, Amazon.com invites other Web site owners to become Associates and sell books on their sites.

Let's say you provide guided trips down the Colorado River. Obviously, people who come to your site enjoy the outdoors. The smart business owner uses the site to build a community of outdoor enthusiasts and adventurers. It is likely that the members of this community also enjoy reading about exploration and outdoor adventures, or need instructive books and guides to whitewater rafting. For most small entrepreneurs, selling books is probably a poor use of capital, given the low margins on book sales and the need to stock inventory that may or may not sell. As an Amazon.com Associate, the small entrepreneur can arrange to sell books on topics appropriate to the business and the tastes of the Web-site community. The orders pass straight through to Amazon.com and earn the Associate a commission. It's a win-win-win strategy. Customers can order books on a topic of interest directly from a familiar site, the business owner can provide greater service to customers while earning a small commission, and Amazon.com broadens its distribution network.

BUY YOUR GROCERIES ONLINE

Peapod, billed on its Web site as "America's #1 Online Grocer," is an example of a business that didn't exist prior to coming online. The original business plan called for: making arrangements with supermarkets in major cities; publishing a list of available groceries, produce, and other products; inviting people in the geographic areas the company served to make their selections and choose what time they wanted their orders delivered; and hiring expert shoppers to fulfill the orders. It was a simple concept. The challenges cofounders Andrew B. and Thomas L. Parkinson faced were cementing arrangements with local markets, providing customers with special software to handle the transactions, and building brand awareness. But the idea seems to be working, albeit with some revisions to the original plan.

Since going online in 1989 as Peapod.com, the Skokie, Illinois–based business has expanded to eight other major metropolitan areas: Austin, Boston, Chicago, Columbus, Dallas/Fort Worth, Houston, Long Island (New York), and San Francisco/San Jose. To date it has signed up more than 100,000 customer members. The supermarkets that support Peapod are impressive too: Stop & Shop in Boston, Randalls in Austin and Houston, Safeway in San Francisco and San Jose, and Kroger in Columbus. For 1998, revenues were up 21.8 percent, to $69.3 million. The business is still operating at a loss, given the money being invested in expansion to new markets, improving technology, the addition of new services, and the acquisition of new members. But those losses are declining, and the opening of a warehouse in Long Island, New York, which enables Peapod to fulfill orders directly at lower prices than by buying through local supermarkets, may prove to be a key to the online grocery model. Growth has been slower than anticipated, largely due to the capital-intensive requirements for building a strong infrastructure. Still, hopes run high; the grocery market today generates hundreds of billions of dollars in revenue every year. To increase its capitalization, Peapod went public in June 1997.

Is Peapod an online community? Well, the site may appear to be less of a community than, say, Amazon.com. During the two years that I've been tracking Peapod, I've watched its Web site change. It's certainly more slick and professional-looking today, but during the early years of building the brand it strove primarily to build a community of food lovers. Whether you were a member or not, the site invited you in to view recipes and follow links to a variety of culinary-related sites.

The real power of Peapod lies in the convenience it offers, without sacrificing quality or price. Members can select from thousands of name-brand products—the same ones they buy in their local markets. Because customers can retrieve any of their last three shopping lists and add or subtract from that list to create a new list, they save additional time ordering. Customers can closely monitor their spending too, since the shopping list maintains a running total; and any coupons and specials available in the store are honored online.

Want to know if online shopping is available in your area? Enter your zip code at the Web site, and they'll tell you. Alas, my hometown is not covered; but Peapod is still growing, and I continue to hold out hope. In the meantime, Peapod offers other services designed to help expand the brand and bring in additional revenue. The company recently announced Peapod Packages, which will drop-ship dry goods anywhere in the United States. The plan, in part, is to use this service to prepare specialty bundles (care packages for students or campers away from home, new-baby bundles, and a variety of gourmet gifts) that customers can order online. Many experts in this field believe that the specialty item market may generate greater opportunity than grocery sales, and that customers will be more receptive to the service charges and monthly fees when sending or requesting special products than when ordering their grocery staples.

Peapod also tracks shopping patterns and uses the data to test-market special offers to its clients. For a fee, this research is also made available to other consumer goods companies, but steps are taken to protect the privacy of individual customers.

Four years ago, Peapod supported Internet access, but management encouraged its customers to use direct modem access through an 800 number. Given the technology most pervasive in the marketplace at the time, the company believed that direct access would provide customers with the fastest link to the Peapod shopping application. Peapod has grown considerably since then, and today Internet access is the primary connection.

Peapod exemplifies the timelessness of the most basic online marketing issues. The Peapod approach to building a business is a model for success in a technology-intensive environment. The way it does business has matured, but the emphasis on providing value—convenience, quality service, speed, and ease of use—still stands as the key ingredient of the firm's success.

MARKETING 1 TO 1

FIGURE 2-1 Marketing 1 to 1's Web site home page.

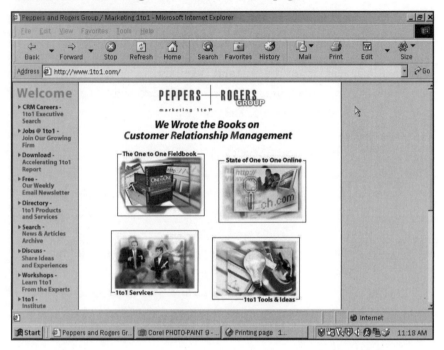

Can a highly promotional Web site also be an online community? I think so, and I believe that Don Peppers and Martha Rogers's Marketing 1 to 1 (www.1to1.com) is a perfect example. It's an excellent example of a promotional site designed to build business and, at the same time, promote a business theory: relationship management.

You've heard that there is strength in numbers. Well, Peppers and Rogers have put this concept to work for their business. While they promote their books and many services, including speaking, consulting, and training, they encourage online discussion and surround themselves with other companies—partners, clients, and directory listings—that subscribe to the principles of one-to-one marketing. Viewing the list of participating firms strengthens the notion that there is real merit in relationship management. The Directory Listing, which charges companies for Profile or Snapshot listings, provides additional revenue to support the site. At the same time, this service makes the site that much more valuable to clients and other visitors.

Peppers and Rogers then build on this support in several ways. They offer to send their free monthly newsletter (actually an e-letter) to anyone who signs up. You can download interactive tools that enable you to make assessments about your business and its capacity to benefit from a one-to-one marketing approach that advocates the "lifetime value of customers." These tools are based on techniques described in Peppers and Rogers's book *Enterprise One to One.* You also can download video clips from past presentations by both Peppers and Rogers; and they've added a special online seminar that you can view at your convenience. The program, called "Marketing One-to-One: Personalizing Every Call Center Interaction," features presentations by the company's principals as well as academics and top people from other companies that practice the principles of one-to-one marketing.

The Web site does not actually handle financial transactions online, but it includes sign-up forms, to which employees of the Peppers and Rogers Group respond. This is a truly artful site. It has recently been redesigned with a layout that clearly displays the full range of offerings available. If I were to find any fault with the site, it would be the lack of true one-to-one delivery of site content. Still, the site is very convenient and easy to use. Every section can be searched, which certainly enables visitors to find exactly the information they want. In the section called "60-Second Overviews," visitors can select the category that best describes the size and type of business they have. But all the information is generic, including the monthly e-letter.

A site that fully employs technology to create a true one-to-one marketing relationship like Amazon.com offers would be expensive and possibly beyond the means of a $12 million firm. But it's a concept to keep in mind and apply in little ways whenever possible.

WAXMAN CAMERA

FIGURE 2-2 Waxman Camera's Web site home page.

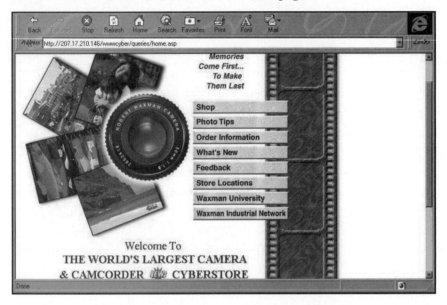

When I first began studying e-commerce, I discovered and became a devotee of the Robert Waxman Camera site. In its 40 years in the business, Robert Waxman Inc. has grown to become one of the largest camera distributors in the United States, with retail outlets in Colorado. Waxman's Web site, billed as the World's Largest Camera Cyberstore, did virtually everything right:

- *It listed the many advantages up front*—huge inventory, lowest prices, years of experience, and the ability to ship anywhere in the world.

- *It offered added value to visitors* by providing photography tips and advice.

- *It allowed visitors to enjoy plenty of graphical sizzle* using state-of-the-art animation, but only when they wanted to select that option. Those who had slow modems or were in a hurry to order weren't forced to wait through long graphic downloads.

- *It kept text to a minimum.* It was a point-and-click site that was highly interactive. All the information a customer could want was available, but only when and as requested. The customer was not hit with information overload up front.

I write about the Robert Waxman Camera site in the past tense because in October 1998, the large Atlanta-based Wolf Camera acquired Waxman Camera and incorporated it into Wolf's fast-growing enterprise that includes a nationwide chain of stores and a Web site. Waxman's Web site is gone, but its business case for e-commerce is so unique it deserves inclusion here. Ross Leher, former president of Waxman Camera, is currently applying his novel concept to a global start-up, described later in this book. First, let's look at Waxman's innovations:

The greatest weakness of any retail enterprise is not having enough knowledgeable staff. Although Waxman's 300 employees represented some of the best in the business, the frequency with which products change and new cameras and features are introduced makes it difficult for even the best people to stay informed. Furthermore, when a manufacturer's inventory is large, it is virtually impossible for a buyer to evaluate the complete product line.

The solution? Develop an interactive, online system built on the best in-house expertise and a comprehensive database. Through an easy-to-use front end, customers could identify products by listing the features, brands, and price range they wanted.

The pièce de resistance was the electronic form that allowed each customer not only to "build" a camera with the features he or she wanted, but also to list them in order of priority. After making selections based on the type of camera or accessory needed, manufacturer(s) preferred, features, and price range (using a series of simple point-and-click checklists), a "smart" search engine quickly ran these requirements against Waxman's complete inventory of more than 9,800 cameras and accessories and listed all the products that fit the criteria.

Once the customer selected an item from the list, a picture of the product and more detailed information were made available. At this point,

Robert Waxman Camera was ready to take the order and ship it anywhere in the world. From start to finish, this was an intriguing example of using a Web site to provide useful information, service customer needs, and transact business online.

The site had one additional advantage, this one for manufacturers. In the process of serving the buying customer with access to a comprehensive database of cameras and accessories, the system served manufacturers by making sure each company's complete product line was readily available for consumer consideration—an important issue for a seller with such a large inventory. Manufacturers never have to worry that a salesperson would forget about a particular model or refrain from suggesting a particular camera based on his or her individual taste and preferences.

And there was a sense of community about the site. First, the company had 40 years of photographic experience upon which customers could draw. Because virtually every employee was either a professional or serious amateur photographer, visitors benefited from their knowledge. The Photo Tips section included tips on servicing and maintaining your cameras; a glossary of industry terminology; techniques for photographing people, landscapes, and wildlife; and advice on how to prepare and equip oneself for a variety of photographic situations. Three years ago the site included selected pictures taken by employees. This was later replaced with online training, with greater emphasis being placed on techniques for taking better pictures.

DEVELOP YOUR OWN BUSINESS COMMUNITY

Building a community online requires you to spend more time and effort up front, getting to know the members of your target community and what they want in a Web community. Here are ten steps, a series of worksheets, and a sample matrix to help you begin your investigation. They serve as guidelines; they are not set in stone. However, the information in this chapter should help you take the first steps toward creating a useful and successful community.

STEP ONE: LEARN THE BASICS ABOUT WHAT THE INTERNET IS AND HOW IT WORKS

Although a recent commercial phenomenon, the Internet dates back to the early 1970s, when the U.S. Department of Defense's Advanced Research Projects Agency (ARPA), along with several large universities, developed a complex communication network called ARPANet. In the late 1980s, the National Science Foundation expanded access to include more universities, bringing the number of online host systems to 300,000. Compare this with the more than 5 million host systems on the Internet today, and the commercial potential becomes clearer.

Also in the late 1980s, Tim Berners-Lee at CERN, the European Laboratory for Particle Physics, created a network within the Internet, called the World Wide Web, to explore the potential for distributed computing. Today, with more than 4,500 Internet Service Providers in North America alone, each with its own network, the system truly resembles a web. Collectively, these networks and host systems form the Internet.

A series of more than 100 communication protocols, call Transmission Control Protocol/Internet Protocol (TCP/IP), gives each computer connected to the Internet a unique identifying number. Software designed to ensure that all systems speak the same language prepares data for sending and receiving online. A series of routers treat Internet addresses as incoming data and determine whether to keep the data or reroute to another network. Data passes from router to router until it finds its correct location.

STEP TWO: SELECT AN INTERNET SERVICE PROVIDER (ISP)

Your ISP will provide you with a gateway for bringing your site onto the Internet. This firm typically offers services ranging from hosting and server management to design, programming, and technical skills. The more you know what to expect from an ISP, the better equipped you will be to interview companies and find the one that's right for you. If you haven't yet decided where your site should reside (on a server in your office or at the ISP's office), your ISP can help you make this decision by providing cost models and a list of the technical skills you will need in either case.

CHECKLIST FOR SELECTING AN ISP

Before selecting an Internet Service Provider (ISP), check on the quality and range of services available to you. With price being very competitive today, the difference may just lie in the tools, services, and access an ISP has...or lacks.

- *Points of Presence.* Determine whether your ISP offers a local phone number in your town or city. If not, you might be subject to higher connection charges. If you travel, determine the national coverage you can expect. Will you have access to your e-mail and the Internet when you're on the road? While you might not find a local number for every town, you ought to be able to call a neighboring city, which will be cheaper than calling the number you use at home. The largest providers offer local numbers coast to coast and, increasingly, are adding international access for a nominal fee. Some even offer 800 numbers. Having a large selection of numbers to choose from may also help you find a free line, even during the high-traffic hours.

- *Web Hosting.* If you're planning to have your ISP host your Web site, ask for a complete rundown on their setup (number of servers, typical size of files they handle, support for online transactions, and backup and security strategies). Then ask the ISP to price out all the features. For example, what is the cost to add online transaction processing? Also ask about your Web address. If they typically provide space on their company server, will you be required to use a naming convention, such as www.theircompany.com/your company? Or do you have the option to use your own URL, such as www.yourcompany.com?

- *Toll-Free Access.* For times when you are away from local numbers and can't or don't want to incur a phone charge, it's good to have the option of toll-free access. Remember, many hotels tack on a surcharge, even for local calls.

- *Technical Support.* From time to time you may decide to add new software and features, such as an e-mail management program or transaction processing. Problems occasionally arise, and you want to know that you'll get the support and access to expertise you need. Because the phone wait for support lines can be long, you may want to find a company with toll-free service (or guaranteed quick response).

- *Value-Added Tools and Services.* If you need help developing your site and don't know whom to hire, look for an ISP that offers more than the basic hosting and maintenance services. Does the ISP provide templates for quick (often less-expensive) Web site design? Can they provide in-house experts to help you, or recommend good designers? Does the ISP support a database or template format, and are the prices competitive? Shop around to see what kinds of tools and services are available.

- *Ease of Use.* How user friendly is your ISP? Is the system easy to access? Do they make it possible for you to update content on your site remotely? Being able to do this, can save you considerable expense.

STEP THREE: SPEND TIME FAMILIARIZING YOURSELF WITH ANY EXISTING WEB COMMUNITIES IN YOUR BUSINESS OR INDUSTRY

If you find sites selling products and services that compete with your own offerings or well-developed Web sites that cater to your prospective customer base, you need to determine:

TIP:

Even if the traffic counter on a site is inflated, you can get a good idea of the amount of traffic by writing down the visitor count on your first visit. Then monitor the number on subsequent visits over a period of days, weeks, or even months. Think of it as a Web site's odometer.

- How large is their customer base, membership list, or click-through rate? Often you can find this kind of information by reviewing information about the company, press releases, and the counters designed to track the number of site visitors.

- Compare the size of their customer-prospect-visitor base with industry estimates for your field.

- Analyze the quality of the content: Is it accurate? Comprehensive? Well-written? Useful?

- What are they selling? How do their product and service offerings compare with your own?

- Do the site owners appear to have any interesting and value-added offerings that may be the result of associations, joint ventures, relationships with direct competitors, or vertically related services and products?

- Is the site easy to navigate? Logical? Easy to read?

- How effectively do your competitors market themselves and their products or services?

- Would you feel compelled to buy from them? Is so, why? If not, why not?

FIGURE 3-1 This worksheet will help you capture competitive information. Then use this information to formulate ways to challenge each competitor.

Site	Traffic	Ease of Navigation	Value-Added Features	Quality and Types of Content	Products and Services Sold
Competitor 1					
How You Plan to Compete					
Competitor 2					
How You Plan to Compete					
Competitor 3					
How You Plan to Compete					

FIGURE 3-2 These are a few of the basic criteria any business owner must consider. As you collect ideas, keep a log that you can refer to later.

Company &URL	Objective	How well objective is met	Best features	Worst features	Value-added features	Would you return?

Whether this will be your first Web site or you are ready to rethink and redesign your original effort, the best resource for ideas is the Web itself. You can learn much about trends in design, what works and what doesn't, just by looking at other Web sites. The more analytical your evaluation, the more prepared you'll be to develop an effective Web site of your own. Here are ten small business sites to get you started on your voyage of discovery:

The Great American Office, LLC	www.gaos.com
FashionMall	www.fashionmall.com
Marketing 1 to 1	www.1to1.com
Alexander Communications	www.alexander-pr.com
DirectCom Inc.	www.directcom-inc.com
Bowne Internet Solutions	www.bowneinternet.com
GT Bicycles	www.gtbicycles.com
J'antiques & Collectibles	www.jantiques.com
Ty Inc.	www.ty.com
Verandah Sportsware	www.verandahsport.com

As you put each site through its paces, ask yourself: How well does this site function? How effectively does it capture my interest and answer my questions? What is the business objective, and has it been met? Most important, would I come back to the site again?

STEP FOUR: JOIN AN EXISTING COMMUNITY

You may decide that the best route will be to join an existing Web community where you can learn by example. With a better understanding of the opportunities an online community can afford and the realization that it is within the reach of every business owner, you can focus on the products and services you want to offer online...and how to best present them to consumer and business prospects. As you study communities, keep asking yourself: What value do they provide? Do I feel comfortable and compelled to participate? Does it fulfill my needs?

FIGURE 3-3 What works for you? Another very good way to help you focus on what works online is to study in depth the communities that impress you the most. Use this worksheet to list five communities that impress you, and explain why. Later you may decide to adapt some of these elements for your own site.

1. Site: Why:
2. Site: Why:
3. Site: Why:
4. Site: Why:
5. Site: Why:

STEP FIVE: BUILD A PROFILE OF YOUR IDEAL CUSTOMER

The more you know about the people you want to reach, the better you can serve their needs and specifications for information, products, and services. Start with a demographic profile. Determine their age, income, jobs or professions, education, and so on. Be as thorough as you can. Remember to include a profile of both your current customer base and your ideal customer. If the two profiles do not match, you'll have to decide whom it is you want to reach. Among your options, you can decide to:

- Concentrate on prospects that match your current customer profile, since they are proven buyers;

- Upgrade your customer base to match your ideal profile; or

- Expand your reach by catering to both profiles simultaneously.

If you decide on the third option, you'll need to make it easy for each profile group to find the information, services, and products that are appropriate to their purchasing profiles.

Other questions to ask to determine usage habits and patterns are: Are your customers more likely to access your site at home or at work? Are your customers looking for product and service information; general knowledge about your business or industry; entertainment; or edutainment (an educational experience that is fun to use)? The last category is most often associated with youthful users, but it can also have a place in business sites. Everyone enjoys a game; just don't overdo the fun to the point that you lose focus on the learning aspect.

Determine whether the customer base you are attracting to your community is well-informed or inexperienced. You'll need to match your presentation of content to people's knowledge and experience. If they have expertise, you'll want to develop ways to tap that knowledge, such as discussion forums or chat rooms.

Remember that this is an ongoing process. You must never stop trying to learn more. You must always be adding depth, refining your knowledge, and applying it to your site design and content. Once your site is up and running, invite your visitors to tell you what they like and want, but be prepared to respond. Nothing is more frustrating than providing your advice and opinions, only to have them ignored. Consider making a general policy statement to the effect that all ideas are reviewed and those most commonly requested are being built into the site.

FIGURE 3-4 Use this sample worksheet to list specific attributes of your current and ideal customer profiles.

Attributes	Current Customer	Ideal Customer
Age		
Education		
Job/Career/ Profession		
Income		
Hobbies		
Other		

FIGURE 3-5 Start with the information in the customer profile worksheet, and fill out the additional columns. Your plan is beginning to take shape.

Attributes	Current Customer	How You Plan to Serve Current Customers Online	Ideal Customer	How You Plan to Serve Ideal Customers Online
Age				
Education				
Job/Career/ Profession				
Income				
Hobbies				
Other				

STEP SIX: IDENTIFY THE CONTENT, TOOLS, AND SERVICES THAT WILL BEST SERVE YOUR CUSTOMERS AND PROSPECTS

Once you have identified your customer, consider the types of content you will need to offer and the most appropriate format. Enter your ideas into the How You Plan to Serve columns of the chart in Figure 3-5.

Are there any interactive tools or calculators that will help your customers in their jobs or make their buying decisions easier? Be creative.

- A real estate community might provide customers with an estimating or (unofficial) appraisal tool that helps them determine the price range of a home they are considering buying or selling.

- A computer manufacturer or network design service might create a tool that helps prospective customers determine what they need (e.g., memory, CPU speed, monitor type, number of network hubs) to accomplish a desired set of tasks or run a particular application.

- An interior design community might sell wallpaper or paint. The members would probably appreciate a utility that helps them select the right products for their needs or calculates how much paper or paint they will need to order for a particular project.

Next, consider the distribution of your content. What services and information do you want to make available free of charge? Which items do you feel require you to set a usage fee? In making these decisions, you need to calculate the cost of doing business, your budget for acquiring new customers, and your advertising budget. Sometimes the cost and effort of promoting and administering something that will bring in little added revenue, relative to your regular products and services, is best given away. Chalk these items up to the cost of doing business. Think of these products or services as loss leaders that will encourage customers to buy items with a higher profit margin. On the other hand, if you have a proprietary tool with tremendous potential, such as an online business plan writer, treat it like a product and set a fee for its use.

Remember to focus on content, services, and online features that provide added value not available through traditional business channels, including storefronts. The key is to provide convenience, useful information, a higher level of customer service, and speed (which translates to time saved online).

STEP SEVEN: DESIGN AN ONLINE ENVIRONMENT THAT MAKES ALL ELEMENTS EASY TO USE AND EASY TO FIND, AND THAT MAKES VISITING THE SITE A PLEASANT AND REWARDING EXPERIENCE FOR YOUR TARGET COMMUNITY

- Select fonts and type sizes that are clear and easy to read.

- Avoid overly cluttered or complex backgrounds that make it difficult to read the text.

- Try to limit your use of graphics, video, and audio that provide value. Your site need not be sterile to function. Just don't allow these elements to get in the way of doing business.

- Create a layout that makes it easy to find everything. Your site can be chock full of resources; just make certain that what you have to offer never appears overwhelming. A good designer can be a real asset here.

TIP

View your site like a typical customer would. Whether you or a professional Web designer builds the site, try viewing it on several different computer systems (including both IBM-compatible and Apple Macintosh platforms). Look at the site using different versions of both the Microsoft Internet Explorer and Netscape browsers. Also, try to view your site using computers with different modem speeds and a range of screen sizes. Finally, invite employees, friends, and colleagues to view the site before it goes live. A second or third set of eyes may spot a flaw you missed.

- Provide a site map and search tool, and don't bury them on the page. You're not trying to send your visitors on an Easter egg hunt.

STEP EIGHT: DEVELOP METRICS AND TOOLS TO MEASURE RESULTS THAT WILL HELP YOU EVALUATE THE SUCCESS OF YOUR COMMUNITY

Measurement tools are best built into a Web site's original design. If you think you can't afford to spend the money now, you may be unhappily surprised when you receive the bill for the redesign later. Here are a few metrics you may find useful:

- *Track how many people visit your site.* How long do they stay? What do they spend the most time doing? If they spend more time trying to get your interactive tools to work, maybe something is wrong with your design. If they spend more time reading and shopping, you are probably on target.

- *Set realistic goals you can use to benchmark your results.* Unless you know what you want to accomplish, you won't know whether you are meeting your objectives or not. For example, how many new customers do you need each month to justify the expense of developing and maintaining the site? At what point does online revenue surpass the total costs associated with building and maintaining the site? What percentage of your revenue do you hope to generate through online sales?

- *Track the number of visitors who become members, customers, or repeat visitors.* Setting up this measurement requires programming expertise that you'll probably need to rely on a professional site developer or programmer for, but it is the best way to determine the effectiveness of the site.

- *Tracking frequency of visits.* In other words, how often do people return to the site? What's the time lapse between visits? Do they visit three or four times and then disappear forever? If so, you may not be updating your site often enough. On the other hand, yours may be a seasonal busi-

ness. In that case, you may want to determine whether any drops in frequency online parallel activity in your offline business. With this information, you can decide whether your online business requires a larger
marketing effort or a special off-season sale to stimulate business.

STEP NINE: PLAN FOR THE FUTURE

As your site grows, and it will, you will want to expand within a preconceived plan. If you don't make allowances for future growth, your site will
appear tacked together, like a house with three or four clashingly different
architectural styles. At some point, changes will become extensive enough
that you will need to redesign. But if you build enough room and flexibility into your design to accommodate future additions, you can expect your
initial site design to last 12 to 15 months.

- You don't have to launch every department, every tool, and every
  product or service the first day you go online, but you do need to set
  up a schedule for their development and release.

- If you plan to expand your site dramatically during the first year, factor these expectations into your planning phase. Leave room in your
  site design for the additions you expect to make.

- Create an editorial calendar for adding new content—and stick to it.
  The more often you update your site, the better. Create a schedule that
  is realistic and that you or your staff can perform without becoming
  overburdened.

STEP TEN: MONITOR YOUR SITE'S ACCESSIBILITY

All your work to develop a business community online will be for nothing
if your site is inaccessible much of the time. If your ISP has trouble with its
equipment and shuts down the server hosting your site, then no one can log
on to your site. In other words, your business is closed. You'll have to

accept some degree of downtime. ISPs occasionally replace systems, upgrade their software, and perform standard maintenance chores. But if their repairs and upgrades are getting in the way of your ability to do business, something is wrong.

Monitor your site's accessibility by logging on. Encourage your employees to do the same, and ask customers to tell you if they are having problems getting to your site.

FIGURE 3-6 This worksheet will help you begin to formulate a set of benchmarks. You may decide to test your benchmarks more often than I have suggested.

Goals	6 months	1 year	2 years	3 years
Number of visitors per month (frequency)				
Number of leads generated online				
Number of online customers				
Revenue projections				
Cost to acquire a customer				
When do you expect to make a profit online?				
Cost to build the site				
Cost to maintain the site				

FIGURES 3-7, 3-8, AND 3-9 Here is an example of a three-month schedule. It's probably more ambitious than anything you'll want to try, but it illustrates how the process works.

Month 1

Monday	Tuesday	Wednesday	Thursday	Friday	Saturday	Sunday
1 new headline add content case study	2 open new discussion topic	3 new headline	4 update/add tool or utility	5 new headline	6	7
8 new headline add content	9 Update FAQs	10 new headline	11 change home page graphics	12 new headline	13	14
15 new headline add content case study	16 open new discussion topic	17 new headline	18 update "What's New"	19 new headline	20	21
22 new headline add content	23 Update FAQs	24 new headline	25 update/add tool or utility	26 new headline	27 change home page graphics	28
29 new headline add content case study	30 open new discussion topic	31 new headline				

Month 2

Monday	Tuesday	Wednesday	Thursday	Friday	Saturday	Sunday
			1 change home page graphics	2 new headline	3 update/add tool or utility	4
5 new headline add content	6 open new discussion topic	7 new headline	8 Update FAQs	9 new headline	10 update "What's New"	11
12 new headline add content case study	13 update/add tool or utility	14 new headline	15 change home page graphics	16 new headline	17	18
19 new headline add content	20 open new discussion topic	21 new headline	22 Update FAQs	23 new headline	24	25
26 new headline add content case study	27 update "What's New"	28 new headline	29 change home page graphics	30 new headline		

Month 3

Monday	Tuesday	Wednesday	Thursday	Friday	Saturday	Sunday
					1	2
3 new headline add content	4 open new discussion topic	5 new headline	6 update/add tool or utility	7 new headline	8 update "What's New"	9
10 new headline add content case study	11 Update FAQs	12 new headline	13 change home page graphics	14 new headline	15	16
17 new headline add content	18 open new discussion topic	19 new headline	20 update/add tool or utility	21 new headline	22	23
24 new headline add content case study	25 Update FAQs	26 new headline	27 change home page graphics	28 new headline	29 update "What's New"	30
31 new headline add content						

4

IS PORTAL STATUS A REASONABLE GOAL?

The portal, also called destination site, may be the most misunderstood and misused concept on the Internet today. The size of a site and the number of visitors and customers it attracts are often used to define a site as a portal. Go to the Web site Inmaze, "The Family of Web Portals" (www.inmaze.com), to find links to a number of fine sites. In contrast to this site, most of the so-called portals are really vertical and horizontal business sites supporting customers' needs for gifts, pets, fitness, and other categories.

True portal stature is less a matter of size than a function of the ability to serve as a user's primary home base online. Having a large inventory of goods and services to sell has very little to do with achieving portal stature. It should be a given that you will meet your customers' expectations in terms of product. Even having a large base of members, customers, or regular visitors online does not automatically elevate a site to portal stature. Rather, a portal is a site set up to support the most basic Internet services of its members, subscribers, customers, and regular visitors. These services include e-mail, online calendar functions, custom news pages, member chat rooms, a stock ticker and personal portfolio manager, and a search engine, to name a few. Recently, portals have started offering online tools and templates to help people create small personal or business Web sites, which are then hosted on the portal's server. Usually the many services are provided free of charge in an effort to secure the loyalty and regular visitation of the prospective customer.

Here are five areas that will need your attention if you want to create a true Web portal:

- *Focus on being the primary site* for a large base of repeat visitors and members, which you can use to attract advertising dollars and lucrative marketing relationships. This is not to say that sales cannot be an important objective.

- *Focus on people, not profits, in the early stages.* The stakes are growing every day, and you must acquire millions of regular visitors in order to capture the interest of advertisers and businesses looking for joint ventures, acquisitions, and co-marketing relationships. Develop a business plan that can sustain you through a period when you will probably lose money. To become a portal today, you need to move quickly to capture people's "eyes" and minds. Gradual growth really is not an option. Too many other Web site owners have the same objectives; you need to be better and faster than your competition.

- *Focus on acquiring capital.* To support a business model that loses money, you need deep pockets or access to millions in venture capital. If you don't plan to fund this venture out of your own purse, you should have a very creative idea, solid plans for managing operations, and a business plan that demonstrates both your knowledge of the market (and its potential) and your efforts to perform the necessary due diligence. You may have heard stories of venture capital firms eager to throw money at anything with a "dot com" in the name. While this is true in some cases, and billions of dollars are being pumped into Internet ventures, this situation won't last forever. When the disappointments and lost investments start piling up—and they will—the feeding frenzy will be over, and only those people with good solid plans will have a chance at gaining venture support.

- *Focus on the features and functions available on your site.* You must provide the basic services—such as free e-mail, search engine, calendar functions, etc.—and then go beyond this to provide additional (and, if possible, unique) tools and functions that will appeal to the broadest base of your target market. You want to come across as the one essential site your members, customers, and subscribers need to visit, and visit often.

- *Focus on promoting your site.* To attract the large numbers of visitors you'll need to make this model succeed, you need to be prepared to spend hundreds of thousands, and maybe millions, on marketing and advertising promotion. If your target market is unaware of your presence or doesn't view your services as essential, you will fail.

On the Internet, viewers are everything. Companies with portal aspirations hope to translate their ability to capture people's eyes into advertising dollars and lucrative co-marketing agreements. Because a user really only needs one portal, the battle to succeed and capture the most eyes is generating a feeding frenzy of online mergers and acquisitions. The leading providers of content are busy snapping up the established portals, and vice versa. In recent months, Disney has acquired 43 percent of search-engine site InfoSeek, and NBC has garnered CNET's Snap! In some cases, portals acquire other portals in a scramble to add popular content and boost their user bases. Hence, AOL acquired Netscape, @Home has Excite, and Yahoo! has been on an acquisition binge.

The fact that most Web users require only one portal site—a central site where they send and receive e-mail, check their calendar, and so on—means that success in this area will be limited to a very few sites. For this reason, most entrepreneurs' business strategies probably will be best focused on creating vertical appeal. If you develop a Web site that fulfills enough of a customer's wants and needs, you may succeed in becoming a large and significant vertical business community. These sites can be created to attract either consumer or professional customers. If your site attracts a large customer base, you can still enjoy the benefits of advertising revenue and co-marketing relationships.

VENTURE CAPITAL FOR E-BUSINESSES

If you have great aspirations for a business venture online but lack the capital to get it off the ground, you may find help among the venture capital (VC) groups. Pricewaterhouse Coopers LLP reports that venture capital available for Web investments grew to $3.5 billion in 1998. That's an increase of 66 percent above the $2.1 billion invested in 1997. How significant is this? The fact is, the VC money invested in 1998 surpassed the $2.8 billion raised in Internet IPOs by almost a billion dollars.

Before you begin looking for venture capital online, first make sure you have a strong business plan that you are willing to share with prospective investors. Second, be prepared to eventually relinquish control of your business in exchange for a healthy buyout. If you are emotionally attached, think of the business as your "baby," and want to retain complete control, then do not invite venture capitalists to the table. Their investment strategy is to earn large returns in exchange for their start-up or growth dollars. You will put in some money and many hours of sweat equity, but this may not be enough to secure control.

If you still feel the urge to explore venture capital, here are a few sites that may help you get started:

- OffRoad Capital Corporation (www.offroadcapital.com)

- Venture Capital HandiLinks (ahandyguide.com/cat1/v/v32.htm)

- InvestorLinks.com (www.thewebinvestor.com/online-venture-directory.html)

So is the difference between a portal or destination site and a vertical business community one of semantics? I don't think so. Differentiating the two plays an important role in your planning right from the beginning. Understanding your objectives up front helps you have a clearer grasp of what you want to accomplish online, whom you want to attract to your site, and how much capital will be required to succeed. A portal has broad-based appeal, provides horizontal services, and gives away basic services, many free of charge. A vertical business community is more focused on a particular slice of the market, a group of shoppers and buyers who generally share the same set of needs and interests. The site is so comprehensive in fulfilling the needs of this target audience that it becomes the first place customers go when they need specific information, services, and products.

By this definition, I would describe a site like CPAnet (www.cpalink. com) as a vertical community designed to serve the needs of professional accountants. It is an excellent site, so rich in resources, information, and links that it is probably one of the first stops for many accountants online. While it includes links to a wide range of key services, tools, calculators, and financial information, most of these functions are not actually built into the site. CPAnet identifies their existence and provides hotlinks to the information and tools. Nor are the basic member services such as e-mail, a calendar, or a search engine included. A user still must establish a portal presence elsewhere to gain access to these Web basics.

Even as a vertical community, achieving top-of-mind stature will require large amounts of capital. You'll need a large and diverse site, which you'll need to update on a continuing basis. Marketing and advertising dollars are essential to making your presence online known; prepare to spend thousands and possibly tens of thousands, and in some cases more. You'll need to be fast on your feet to develop relationships with as many other companies as possible that can add to the richness and comprehensiveness of your site. Finally, you'll want to find a business opportunity that is not already staked out and well served by another vertical community. If you succeed, the return can be tremendous. You'll have access to a large database of prospective customers, which will attract the interest of other companies that want to reach your customers through advertising and direct product sales. Along the way, your site may become an acquisition target, which can mean a lucrative buyout or a large infusion of capital.

While finding the right venue for your community or portal is challenging, just apply your creativity to the task. That, combined with long hours spent online looking at what's being done, will help you identify a niche. Because virtually all the well-known vertical business sites are focused on the consumer market, the greatest opportunity may be in the business-to-business market. Consider this: During a presentation at the Internet Commerce Expo in March 1998, Jeff Papows, the CEO and president of Lotus Corporation, estimated that during the subsequent two years business-to-business commerce would grow to $150 billion. More recently, Forrester Research Inc. projected that the business-to-business market would hit $1.3 trillion by the year 2003. Given that business-to-business sales are expected to dwarf consumer shopping for the foreseeable future, it may be the area with the best success potential.

DISTRIBUTION IS KEY TO BECOMING A PORTAL

Most of the leading portals and destination sites today have their roots in search engine and directory services. This is certainly the case with Yahoo!, but more important is the vision behind the growth. This vision started with cofounders David Filo and Jerry Yang and included two of the earliest employees: Tim Koogle, now Yahoo!'s chairman and CEO; and Jeff Mallett, president and COO. Collectively, they built a business model in 1995 that continues to serve them well today. Tim Koogle shares his insight into this unique business model:

> KOOGLE: *It all started when Jerry and David started keeping track of Internet sites that interested them. They put their list up on one of the Stanford University servers. It wasn't long before friends were asking them to keep track of stuff they liked, then friends of friends were asking, and it just kept expanding. In order to catalog all these sites, Jerry and*

David built a structure. It gained popularity quickly, because it solved a fundamental problem: how to take a very large and growing set of distributed content that lacks any sort of road map and help people find the information they want. They solved that need by starting with a table of contents (or front-of-the-book) approach, as opposed to a more techie, full-text search (back-of-the-book or index) approach.

Our first formal business and operating plan was finished in July 1995. We started bringing in revenue in August and were profitable in September. By April 1996, we were ready to go public, and we've been growing ever since.

AUTHOR: *I think it might surprise some of our readers to learn just how quickly you started to make a profit. We know there have been some major success stories on the Internet. But we also all know of businesses with huge expectations that fell flat on their faces. Can you explain your business model in generic terms?*

KOOGLE: *We designed the business exclusively for the Internet, with a focus on content aggregation and distribution. The Internet is a new platform for distribution of original content or, for that matter, re-purposed content. If you author good quality content and get it in front of people for whom it's relevant, they will consume it. Getting it in front of them means getting it distributed.*

Many distribution gateways exist on the Internet, Yahoo! being one of them. As an original content company, you need to build relationships with as many gateways as possible. Partner with distribution gateways that reach your demographics and you increase the probability that relevant viewers will see your content and consume it. In short, distribution is one way business is shaking out on the Internet. We provide distribution to our content and service partners and navigation to our users.

AUTHOR: *But when you have the content, and it's good, how do you select from the many different gateways available?*

KOOGLE: *The longer this medium is around, the easier it becomes, thanks to mergers and acquisitions and evolution. In 1995 we recognized the value of word of mouth in the Web community, and the network effect that kicks in as the numbers start to grow. It just seems to go around and builds on itself. In developing a short list of gateways to partner with, we looked for companies that were, through their own efforts, attracting large groups of users. The natural partners for us became those Internet service providers (ISPs) and Internet access providers (IAPs) that were establishing a very large-scale business by adding value—bundling services and content with the access.*

In the years that have followed the decision to delineate Yahoo! as a content aggregator, we have developed thousands of partnerships.

CREATING A VERTICAL BUSINESS COMMUNITY

While technically speaking many of the vertical business-to-business and business-to-consumer communities have been staked out already, the hold on these categories is tenuous at best. Whether you are interested in becoming the primary online player in medical and dental supplies, business research, hobbies, business turnaround consulting, oil rig technology, or gardening, there probably is still an opening—and a chance for you to capture the lead.

To accomplish your goal, you literally have to take apart the competition. You need to know everything possible about the size of their markets, the relationships they have developed, the breadth of content they offer, and the products and services they sell. Once you have digested all this information about the competition, you can start your own creative process and come up with a more comprehensive package of offerings, more compelling content, or a better response to the needs of the target market. To see how the process works, let's follow the development of one hypothetical vertical business community:

Our goal is to extend the reach of our current brick-and-mortar auto parts store without opening a chain of retail outlets or moving to a franchise model.

We have used market indicators to determine where our online opportunity exists; now it's time to look at the competition. This is the final, critical piece of market research we need. In this hypothetical example, we have performed due diligence and are satisfied that there is a market for selling auto parts online. No one player appears to dominate. But whom can we expect as our competition in the near future, and what will they do to attract online sales?

We start by exploring the top matches presented by several online search engines and directories to see just who is selling online today. Our initial search using Infoseek turned up 39 million matches. This could be enough to discourage even the most optimistic entrepreneur, but we press on. Among the companies with the largest online presence, we find Auto Value Parts (www.autovalue.com), AutoZone (www.autozone.com), East Coast Automotive (www.ecautomotive.com), AutoHaus (www.autohausaz.com), Virtual Auto Parts (www.cruzio.com), Pepboys (www.pepboys.com), and NAPA (www.napaonline.com).

Most of the companies listed have hundreds of offline customer service outlets and retail stores across the country. But it doesn't take long to realize that the companies with chains and franchise relationships are not selling directly. This could hurt the relationships they have spent years building. We've found our first advantage: We will carry none of the baggage of an established franchisor. We have no franchise relationships or storefront operations. We are free to sell directly online. Among the millions of smaller sites, we find a proliferation of niche marketers. These companies are catering to the needs of antique automobile restorers, import car owners, or the owners of specific makes and models (such as Corvette, Jeep, or Volkswagen). As a premium parts retailer, we will not be in direct competition with these sites.

How, then, are our largest online competitors serving customers online? Most have some sort of locator facility to help customers find the nearest retail outlet. A few provide helpful advice on repairing and replacing everything from air conditioning and fog lights to air filters and windshield wipers. This is a feature we want to offer. We make a note to build an archive of "how to" advice and plan to add new tips twice a month.

One of the sites we visit promises "overnight in-store delivery of most hard-to-find parts." This is a service we will need to match. We will require good relationships with our parts' vendors so we can deliver overnight to a customer's home or business. The business aspect is critical: We will want to sell both to consumers and professional auto mechanics, giving us a larger prospective customer base.

None of the retailers we check out appears to offer a newsletter, online or otherwise. If we provide a monthly e-letter (online newsletter), we have a reason to ask visitors to register at our site. This will give us detailed information on our customer and prospect base, which may help us attract lucrative advertising from the major parts manufacturers. As an added incentive to sign up and become a member of our community, we can offer discounts on selected products or a dollars-off coupon on the first order. Our e-letter will enable us to communicate with customers and prospects each month. We can give readers helpful tips, seasonal advice (such as air conditioning care and advice on antifreeze), and special offers and discounts that may bring them back to our site sooner.

Apparently, there is a need for specialized help among the do-it-yourselfers (DIYers). When they are repairing or restoring a vehicle, they don't always know what part they need. For this reason, many sites provide part finders. After a customer has identified the make, model, year, and other attributes of the vehicle, he or she uses a text box to describe in as much detail as possible the problem and the part needed. Experts at the company use this information to determine the exact part required and then respond to the customer via e-mail with price and availability information. We'll need to offer a similar feature to be competitive.

As we look at some of the links these sites provide, we find a wealth of car clubs, automobile organizations, dealers, car-care products, publications, books, and more. We'll contact Amazon.com or Barnes and Noble to arrange to sell automotive repair books on our site. This will bring added convenience and value to the users of our Web site and an additional source of income to us. But let's not stop there. Why don't we host a free classified service and discussion forum for hobbyists? In addition to the new parts we sell, we can help our customers find salvage parts and rebuilt components.

We'll also let them support one another through a discussion forum that encourages hobbyists to share their experiences.

By creating a distinctive logo for our business and inviting anyone with a site that attracts automotive enthusiasts and professionals to set up reciprocal links, we can further promote our business. This will help us build market exposure without too much expense, and extend awareness of our site outside the limitations of our search engines. If we can design a useful utility, we'll encourage Web site owners to use it onsite or download it as well. Maybe we can create a tool that helps identify original paint colors by make, model, and year.

We have begun to identify some of the value-added features that will help make our online auto parts store distinctive. Now we are ready to start designing our site.

Remember, however, that collecting market intelligence is not a one-time exercise. You need to keep apprised of market developments. Check the competition regularly, and reassess your market opportunity several times a year. Then use this information to revise your business plan. Let's get started.

CHAPTER 5

IDENTIFY YOUR MARKET: THE CORNERSTONE OF GOOD WEB DESIGN

Why should you be on the Internet now? There are many reasons to make the move as soon as possible. For example:

- With the Internet growing so quickly, the time to master the medium has come.
- With growing global participation, competition will be coming from new sources.
- Because strategic collaborations can enhance a site, the sooner a company puts together meaningful relationships, the better.
- Because the Internet can give management greater control over its company's messages, it pays to discover how to use it effectively to create a sort of online infomercial.
- With businesses and individuals around the world gaining Internet access, e-mail capabilities and a Web site enable even small businesses to reach a worldwide audience one at a time and cost-effectively.

Despite all these compelling reasons to go online, never make the fact that your competition is already online your sole rationale for developing a Web site. At first blush, this appears counterintuitive. But if you are simply trying to react to the actions of your perceived competition, you could be opening yourself (and your business) to all manner of problems, false steps, and mistakes. First, you may be apt to focus more on the competition than on building an accurate picture of the marketplace and the real opportunities it presents. You may, in turn, never identify the strategies and tactics that will bring you success online. For all your urgency to master this new marketing, sales, and communication medium, you must put in the time and effort required to develop a picture of the market that will show you what to expect so you can meet the challenge. You cannot ignore what your competition is doing, but don't allow their efforts to become your one compelling reason for bringing your business to the Internet.

If you've committed yourself to e-commerce, you've probably selected the market you want to reach and the products or services you wish to sell. Congratulations; you have taken your first step toward building a Web-based business. But you've only just begun the process. Now it's time for you to ask: Who are my customers? What motivates them? Where can they be found online? What percentage of my total customer base is already online? What is my competition doing to reach the same market? How many competitors do I face online?

Knowing the answers to these questions is important to any business' success. On the Internet it is critical. The answers to these and other questions will help you create a sense of community among your viewers. Furthermore, because the Web is still a relatively new medium for commerce, it's important for you to have the data necessary to set realistic expectations for your online business. Without this information, you may underestimate your opportunity and fail to allocate adequate capital to the task. Similarly, you may discover that your customer base is not yet on the Web, which may mean that a large initial expenditure would be premature unless you were prepared to invest the time and money needed to actually pull your prospective customer base to the Internet—and to your site in particular.

So where do we find the answers? In this chapter, we'll discover that in addition to being a medium for promoting and distributing your products and services, the Internet is also a resource rich in market and competitive information. We'll explore some of the techniques you can use to find the answers to the questions asked here and much more. Remember: The better you know your customers and prospects and understand their online behavior, the more business you'll be likely to close.

YOUR PEERS ARE GETTING ONLINE

Early in 1998, Dun & Bradstreet surveyed the owners of 550 small and medium businesses and discovered that, while about half had Internet access, only about a third had Web sites. Further, among those with Web sites, about a third were used for e-commerce (whether or not they actually accepted online payment). This was a dramatic increase from the results of a 1997 survey, when only 5 percent viewed the Internet as a viable medium for business, and this growth continued through 1999.

Cyber Dialogue Inc. and Find/SVP conducted a similar survey at that time and confirmed Dun & Bradstreet's numbers. They found that 37 percent of small and medium businesses were doing some form of business online (although not necessarily e-commerce). Their inquiries, however, also revealed that about a million more small and medium businesses planned to add Internet access in 1998, and about half of them would have their own Web sites.

FINDING YOUR OPPORTUNITIES IN STATISTICS AND DEMOGRAPHICS

Read any business magazine or newspaper and you're bound to find statistics about the Internet. By collecting as many statistics as possible about your marketplace, you can create market and customer snapshots that will help you position your business online. One word of warning: As you study the numbers, you will begin to see discrepancies from one survey to another. Does this mean one study is wrong and another correct? Not necessarily. One of the best ways to use raw data is to determine its relative value. For example, when you look at more than one list of top market categories by sales, determine whether the categories are ranked in the same order. If they are, you may have a meaningful piece of data.

TIP

If you are afraid you may be comparing apples and oranges or if you want clarification on a research study's sampling error, look to IntelliQuest's research tools (www.intelliquest.com/tools). Here you'll find several calculators that will help you improve the margin of accuracy in your analysis of online research. All the tools are available free of charge.

The longer you study the statistics, the more you'll notice how consistently researchers have underestimated online market performance. The fact is, market growth and customer acceptance are occurring faster than even the professionals can anticipate. Therefore, when researchers look three to five years into the future, they are constantly revising their numbers upward. Try to collect the most current data available.

Let's examine some of the market insight we can gain from the raw data we collect online. We'll start with a broad snapshot of the marketplace, then continue to fine-tune that picture by exploring several sectors of the market.

THE NUMBERS CONTINUE TO GROW

The individual numbers are often less important than the trends they suggest. Odyssey's Homefront survey recently released its results: 47 percent of U.S. households with Internet access purchased online in the six months between August 1998 and January 1999. This was up from 37 percent for the period February through July 1998. But the greatest change—and perhaps the most significant aspect of the trend—was in the amount spent. In the six months from February through July 1998, online buyers spent $19.8 million; in the next six months, that total rose to $56.4 million.

Digital Economy Growing Fast

The New York City–based Internet research firm eMarketer reports that 16.8 million U.S. citizens (age 14 and older) have purchased at least one product or service online. These 16.8 million buyers represent about one-third of all Internet users in the United States, but only about 8 percent of the total U.S. population age 14 and older. Further, eMarketer reports that another 33.1 million U.S. citizens are using the Internet to browse and research the items they will eventually buy offline. We will refer to the first group as "buyers" and the second as "shoppers." The shoppers represent an opportunity for the aggressive e-tailer: to turn shoppers into online buyers. Creating a comprehensive picture of the market, identifying your ideal customers, knowing what they want, and planning accordingly can help you meet the online challenge.

In and of themselves, numbers do not tell us much about our market. But adding eMarketer's projection for the years 1999 and 2003 helps us set some expectations of how quickly the market is going to grow. By the end of 1999, online buyers in the United States were expected to reach 36.1 million (or 16.6 percent of the U.S. population). By 2002, the estimated 63.7 million U.S. buyers will represent almost one-third of the U.S. population. This is a significant portion of the market, and will impact the percentage of revenue you can expect to earn online.

The findings of International Data Corporation are in line with eMarketer's figures. IDC expected fully 46 million U.S. consumers to be buying online by the year 2000.

Commerce Secretary William Daley helps us to put Internet growth into perspective. According to a 1999 U.S. Commerce Department report on digital commerce:

- *Internet traffic is doubling every 100 days*, yielding an annual growth rate of more than 700 percent.

- *Just four years after the Internet opened* to general usage, 50 million people were connected.

- *Information technologies have driven* more than 25 percent of real economic growth during the past five years.

- *Business-to-business transactions* on the Internet will likely surpass $300 billion by 2002.

At this rate of growth, retail and business-to-business opportunities should increase rapidly during the next few years. However, we'll need more information before we can determine when our target market will share in this growth. It's imperative to be online now in order to learn how to use the Web most effectively...before all the world is online.

WHERE IS THE CONSUMER RETAIL OPPORTUNITY...TODAY AND TOMORROW?

It's a fact; everything is not selling equally well. The numbers given here are far from comprehensive; they are meant only to help get you started with your own investigation. According to IntelliQuest's World Wide Internet Tracking Study, only books, software, music, and computer hardware have a 10 percent or greater market penetration online. The top eight online markets ranked in order of sales are: books (25 percent), software (18 percent), music

(15 percent), computer hardware (11 percent), clothing and jewelry (8 percent), travel (8 percent), tickets (7 percent), and miscellaneous (6 percent).

According to Forrester Research Inc. in its April 1998 report "On-Line Retail Strategy," the market share can be broken down as follows: computer products (35 percent), travel (26 percent), books and music (7 percent), gifts and flowers (6 percent), and other (26 percent).

Cyber Dialogue (www.cyberdialogue.com) gives us a slightly different snapshot of the top consumer markets. But by estimating the purchasing frequency of the U.S. adult population, the survey enables us to begin assessing our chances for repeat sales in each of the leading categories:

FIGURE 5-1 One particularly encouraging aspect of this Cyber Dialogue data is the fact that in most categories, the "purchased 5+ times" numbers are dramatically larger than the "purchased once" or "purchased 2–4 times" numbers.

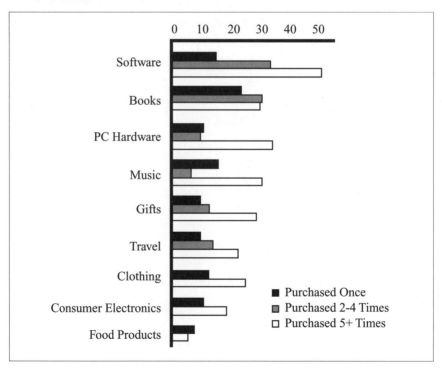

TIP

The numbers for total online revenue may be somewhat inflated, because researchers do not always compare apples with apples. For example, the online retail numbers often include sales figures for service categories (such as travel and online stock trading), which are not included in the offline retail numbers. This need not be a concern, but it is something to take into consideration.

Although the categories in these three studies do not correlate precisely, the lists are consistent enough to suggest the hottest market opportunities today. ActivMedia Research is another source that can help you set your expectations for market growth. In 1998, for example, the revenue from online business-to-business services, telecommunications and broadcasting, travel, distribution, transportation, and wholesale business grew at rates between 100 percent and 149 percent. At the same time, Internet shopping malls and consumer services (not including travel, real estate, and information), as well as business owners using the Web to sell business-to-business products, consumer products, and Internet services, estimated their growth would be between 50 percent and 99 percent of 1997 revenue. (Note: Because online sales still represent a relatively small percentage of total revenue, it doesn't take a lot for the *rate* of growth to seem quite dramatic. For this reason, the numbers are best used to identify areas of relative market strength.)

But where are the future opportunities? Most researchers agree that travel has a strong future in online sales. Even though travel currently represents only about 8 percent of the market, according to IntelliQuest's ebranding study, the dollar amount spent per online transaction actually surpasses the dollar amount spent offline. By 2002, Datamonitor expects the travel industry to account for 35 percent of all online sales. Forrester corroborates this finding and estimates the online consumer travel market will grow to $30 billion by 2003.

Forrester Research Inc. reports a rosy future for consumer buying in the United States, producing an estimated $184 billion by 2004. Worldwide Internet commerce (both consumer and business-to-business) is expected to reach $3.2 trillion by 2003. George F. Colony, president of Forrester Research, told attendees at the 1998 Boston Forrester Forum: "There is no question that iCommerce will represent a significant portion of the global economy over the next five years. To achieve its full potential, businesses need to move quickly to establish market leadership, while governments must nurture electronic commerce with supportive laws and policies. If a favorable climate can be established, Internet commerce will reshape the global economy."

These are encouraging words indeed, but what trends can we uncover? The figures seem to suggest a couple of developments: First, the worldwide market is going to start surpassing U.S. consumption in the next few years; second, business-to-business sales will overshadow consumer sales. This means global opportunities will increase and, while consumer spending receives the best press, the greatest piece of the revenue is going to the business-to-business market. Perhaps this is your market?

ONLINE TRAVEL TRANSACTIONS BEAT THE TRADITIONAL MARKET

	Past 3 Months		**Projected Next 3 Months**	
	Online	Offline	Online	Offline
Travel	$300	$200	$500	$250

Source: IntelliQuest

TIP

Consumer activity can signal business-to-business opportunities. Companies that sell consumer products and services online must rely on other businesses to help them complete secure transactions, communicate with clients, provide superior customer service, and, in many cases, supply the raw materials and products they are selling to consumers. When you find evidence of a market on the verge of hitting it big online, consider how you can serve the businesses in that industry that sell directly to consumers.

Experts at Forrester Research further believe the leading market categories will experience some change in relative value. For example, sales of books and music ($156 million in 1997) are expected to hit $7.5 billion by 2004, while leisure travel is expected to grow from $654 million to $32.1 billion by 2004. This is consistent with the travel market trends we noted earlier. We also learn that apparel and footwear could grow from $92 million in 1997 to $23.6 billion in 2004; ticket sales are expected to grow from $79 million to $3.9 billion; and PC hardware and software from $863 million in 1997 to $158 billion in 2004. All appear to be healthy online markets for retailers, but you'll need to look closely at the existing competition to decide whether any of these are markets you want to enter as a first-time player. If you are already established in one of these industries, the figures suggest that you can expect to attract incremental revenue from an online presence. If you are not established, you will be up against stiff competition.

Another hot market starting to explode online is the field of financial services, specifically banking, insurance, and investment services. Online trading services such as Charles Schwab and e-Trade Securities are picking up new investors at a blinding pace. Charles Schwab reports its clients averaged 153,000 trades in January 1999, (up from 93,000 trades a day during the fourth quarter of 1998. E-Trade added 233,000 new accounts during the first three months of 1999, more than all the accounts added in 1998. Today, almost half of all individual trades are conducted online.

EXPECTATIONS FOR GROWTH

We can attribute the general growth of online activity, in part, to increased online access. But to what do we attribute the growth of e-commerce? It's reasonable to believe that one primary concern of all business owners and consumers is being addressed: security. Certain changes in market procedures had to precede the expansion of e-commerce. Much of the growth appears to be the result of changes in the reality (and perception) of online security:

- *Online entrepreneurs are promoting their use of the newer (and ever-improving) security tools* and services designed to instill increased confidence. Furthermore, they are often backing up their promises of security with guarantees and certifications of safety.

- *The security built into browser technology* and many software applications is continually improving. Companies are increasingly quick to report and fix potential security breaches in their products.

- *As users become more familiar* with the Internet, they feel more comfortable with the notion of conducting business in cyberspace, and they are more confident in the security measures offered. According to the findings of a 1999 *USA Today* poll, 95 percent of those interviewed in the United States reported they were willing to give out their credit card numbers online.

- *Finally, alternatives to credit cards* are beginning to appear on more sites. Among the e-cash systems gradually becoming mainstream are products from CyberCash and the IBM Payment Suite, which includes the IBM Consumer Wallet™ and the IBM Payment Server™ for merchants. With greater support, it is conceivable that some parents will set up accounts (with limits) for their children, enabling them to purchase small-ticket items online.

This is not to say that theft and fraud are absent from the Internet, but only that consumers and businesses are finding the level of risk acceptable.

The popularity of e-commerce is also receiving a boost from the value and comprehensiveness business owners are building into their Web sites. Their sites are more robust, in part due to efforts to make their complete product lines available online. In addition, with what these Web sites have to offer their users in terms of quick response, lightning service, and value-added information, customers actually *want* to do business online.

As a business owner, you need to identify the contributory factors as you see them and apply them to your online efforts.

TIP

To determine your market potential, calculate both the dollars spent on and the savings you enjoy from automation, broader (potentially global) market reach, more efficient and centralized inventory management, and so on. As the online market continues to heat up and your market advantage grows, you may enjoy a higher revenue per employee ratio than traditional retailers.

CAN YOU PROFIT ONLINE?

ActivMedia Research, the Peterborough, New Hampshire research firm that has been collecting Internet data since 1994, reported in a recent annual survey, The Real Numbers Behind Net Profits, that 58 percent of executives who have had sites up and running for three or more years are showing a profit (meaning that revenue exceeds the cost of developing, maintaining, and promoting the site). Across all businesses on the Web, 46 percent claim to show a profit. In 1998, ActivMedia researchers wrote: "Web site annual business revenues now regularly exceed $100k, and in many cases $1 million." Furthermore, they estimated the average business-to-business transaction to be around $3,000.

What percentage of revenue is coming from online sales? When the researchers factored together all online retail sales, ActivMedia estimated that, on average, a business makes about 30 percent of its total revenue through online transactions. About 25 percent of Web-based businesses make more than half their revenue online, but only one in six (about 15 percent) rely on the Web for 90 percent to 100 percent of their revenue. This suggests that the number of exclusively Web-based businesses is still relatively small.

If you are trying to estimate when your Web activities will begin to show a profit, know that the longer your business is online, the better your chances of turning a profit. That extra time online gives your Web-based business time to mature. You can develop a loyal following, continue to build and enhance your Web site, and become more practiced in what it takes to integrate your Web-based activities into all your business planning.

To show a profit, we need to boost revenues while keeping costs as low as possible. One way we can boost revenues is to understand online price barriers. In other words, how much are people willing to spend per transaction? ActivMedia Research reports that:

- One-third of sites sell products under $100.

- Almost another third of sites sell products that cost between $100 and $999.

Research company eMarketer eStats concurs, and calculates the average online purchase to be $162. Only the very low end of the market does not appear to be selling online. Jupiter Communications expects even this trend to change, as e-cash programs and smart cards become pervasive enough to enable customers to sign up easily and use them widely. Jupiter researchers expected that by the year 2000, 80 percent of online transactions would be for items costing less than $10.

SIZE OF RETAIL TRANSACTIONS

Professionals at ActiveMedia Research have broken retail transactions into categories to illustrate the acceptance of various price points by consumers. Note the strength of the $10 to $499 range.

Price	Percent of Transactions
Less than $10	2%
$10–$49	24%
$50–$99	13%
$100–$499	25%
$500–$999	7%
$1,000–$9,999	13%
More than $10,000	4%

What do these statistics suggest? For one thing, it's possible that much of the informational content business owners give away online today—chalking it up to the cost of acquiring customers because the small added revenue is not cost-effective to process—will be available for a small fee. We may also see more pricing models built on low-margin and high-volume sales projections. Finally, we could see new categories of products and services available on the Internet. Selling content is one example, but we may also see several pay-per-view strategies, in which consumers pay small amounts for real-time usage or access. Imagine listening to music or viewing a movie online, or paying to use software online rather than purchasing the software outright.

BUSINESS-TO-BUSINESS OPPORTUNITIES

Whenever we hear about the Internet and e-commerce, whether in the news, in statistical reports, in stock IPOs, or in advertising, the focus is largely on the consumer market. Consumer sales seem to have more appeal and excitement for financial reporters. But the fact is that business-to-business sales will far outdistance consumer spending for several years to come. The New York city–based Internet research firm eMarketer predicts that business-to-business revenue will grow to $268 billion by the year 2002. By way of reference, in 1997, business-to-business revenue was only $5.6 billion. Forrester Research also expects that the pace of growth will increase. By 2003, Forrester expects business customers to be buying $1.3 trillion in hard goods alone through the Internet. Furthermore, the firm's researchers expect online revenue to reach almost 10 percent of total business-to-business sales, which still leaves great room for growth. Starting with the largest market, product sales will be greatest in computing and electronics, followed by motor vehicles, petrochemicals, utilities, paper and office products, shipping and warehousing, food and agriculture, consumer goods, pharmaceutical and medical, aerospace and defense, construction, heavy industries, and industrial equipment.

CREATING A DEMOGRAPHIC PROFILE

We've used the Internet to identify market trends. Next we need to develop profiles of the online shopper and buyer. Again, we'll begin with a broad picture, then try to match this to our ideal customer profile. By virtually all reports, the profile of the typical Internet user continues to come closer to mirroring the public at large. This trend will continue as the number of Internet users worldwide continues to grow.

Even so, it is still fair to say that the typical online consumer is better educated and has more discretionary income than the general public. One change from years' past, however, is that Internet users are now fairly evenly balanced between men and women. In fact, in 1999, 56 percent of first-time Internet buyers were women.

Compiling demographic information from Mediamark Research and CyberStats gives us this picture of the people online:

There is much to be learned from these numbers. For example, if you are selling to the artists, craftspeople, and other people engaged in precision and handicraft work, your market may just be coming online. The number of seniors online is still small.

Gender

Male	53%
Female	48%

Age

18–34	42%
35–54	49%
55+	9%

Education

College graduate	45%
Some college	35%
No college	20%

Occupation

Professional	22%
Management	19%
Clerical/Sales/Technical	28%
Crafts/Repair/Precision	5%
Other	26%

Household income

$150,000+	7%
$75,000-$149,000	33%
$50,000-$74,000	29%
Less than $50,000	31%

Marital status

Single	28%
Married	62%
Other	10%

The online population represents a broad range of interests, hobbies, businesses, and backgrounds. Your challenge is to identify your ideal customer. Note that your definition of a customer can be a consumer, a regular visitor to your site (who you may want to make available to other retailers),

FIGURE 5-2 Mark the checkbox if the category is applicable to your market. When you have checked all categories (or added any new ones), begin to fill out the boxes in each row you checked with data you have collected from research (online and off) and your own experience.

Category	√	Description	Percentage of the Online Market	Other Web Sites Already Serving This Category
Sex				
Male				
Female				
Age				
Teens				
College				
22–27				
Generation X				
Baby Boomer				
Senior				
Education				
High school				
College				
Grad. school				
Professional Deg				
Other				
Income				
Less than $20K				
$20K–$30K				
$31K–$50K				
$51K–$70K				
$71K–$100K				
$100K+				
Access Location				
Work				
Home				

FIGURE 5-2 *Continued*

Category	√	Description	Percentage of the Online Market This Category	Other Web Sites Already Serving
Bus/Industry				
Accounting				
Manufacturing				
Office Admin				
Technology				
Teaching				
Other				
Primary Need				
Parenting				
Business				
Professional				
Career				
Real Estate				
Entertainment				
Other				
Hobbies				
Cooking				
Cars				
Interior Design				
Sports				
Other				

a business-to-business buyer, or an advertiser. It's up to you to set the parameters, then create a demographic profile.

According to an August 1998 survey by ZD Market Intelligence, the number of home and business users is fairly evenly distributed. So whether you are interested in capturing business or consumer customers, the opportunities should exist. Here's a grid to help you begin developing a profile of your ideal audience based on statistical information. Clearly it is only a beginning. You'll want to refine and add to the categories to match your specific requirements.

Women and Minorities Online

The growing online population can be further segmented. For example, not only do we find that women and men are more evenly represented among Internet users, we find that between 1987 and 1996, the number of women-owned businesses in the United States grew by more than 150 percent. These businesses are going online. Cherie Piebes, IBM global market executive for women entrepreneurs, explains: "Fourteen hundred women-owned businesses are started in the United States each day. Rapid adoption of new technology is part of the profile of this group." Data collected at conferences and the annual survey sponsored by IBM and conducted by the National Foundation for Women Business Owners (NFWBO) make a compelling case.

Lois E. Haber, NFWBO chair and president and CEO of Delaware Valley Financial Services, Inc., reports on the latest findings: "Women business owners are using technology to explore new business opportunities." Her organization's findings tell the story:

Internet Usage	Business Owners	
	Male	**Female**
Currently subscribe to online service	41%	47%
Frequently use Internet or e-mail to communicate	40%	51%
Frequently conduct research via the Internet	14%	22%
Use Internet to bid for contracts or review business opportunities	3%	9%

Organizations such as the Office of Women's Business Ownership (OWBO), a branch of the Small Business Administration, recognize Internet training as an important component in their work with women entrepreneurs. Sherrye Henry, assistant administrator of OWBO, has developed a site to handle online conferencing (www.onlinewbc.org) to educate trainers on key business issues for women clients.

With the probability of women reaching an online majority presence in 1999, and given that women are expected to make the majority of purchases for the home, it is important to know how best to reach this market. For example, many people believe that women do not "surf the Web" as much as men. They tend to go directly to their primary sites, so you should remind these customers to bookmark your sites. This will help ensure their return and improve your chances of becoming a favorite site.

Some women favor sites rich in information, including testimonials from other buyers. Some women favor consensus building, so sites that foster online discussion appeal to them.

According to most market research firms, the Web is also becoming more diverse. Forrester Research, for example, finds that Asian Americans have the highest online participation (64 percent are online). The number of African Americans accessing the Web was expected to increase 42 percent in 1999, bringing their total to 40 percent of households. At a 20 percent rate of growth, 43 percent of Hispanic American households were expected to be online by the end of 1999.

Introduce cultural diversity into the images you select for your Web site. If your Web site includes customer testimonials, by all means select examples that are representative of all races, sexes, and cultures.

The Youngest and Oldest Come Online

If your target market includes children or senior citizens, you'll find both groups' online participation growing, and both groups have purchasing power. Although the impact of minors may be more as influencers, there is a trend toward encouraging parents to set up online credit accounts with limitations on how much the children can spend each month.

Many senior citizens, on the other hand, have a high percentage of discretionary income. They also represent a small percentage of the online market. A survey by Microsoft and the American Society on Aging found that while 50 percent of adults in the United States own and use computers, only 24 percent of those 60 and older own and use computers. According to the Mediamark Research and CyberStats, 9 percent of seniors were currently online. We can expect, however, that as baby boomers age, the numbers of seniors online will rise dramatically.

Reach a Worldwide Audience

All your customers may not be U.S. citizens. The growth of Internet use around the world will bring new customers as well as new competition. If you sell products and materials that you import, expect more and more of your suppliers to sell directly to your business and consumer customers. By the same standard, you may benefit from global e-commerce by having greater access to global trading partners and by finding new online markets for your business.

The prospect of doing business with individuals and companies anywhere in the world fuels entrepreneurial interest in electronic commerce. No other communication medium enables so many buyers and sellers to transact business globally via local telephone numbers. During the past few years, while the rate of worldwide growth deserved our attention, the Internet was still a market in the making. We had to focus on future opportunity. That is changing. For example, eMarketer estimates an annual growth rate of 70 percent in the non-U.S. online market during the next five years. By 2002, its researchers predict, more than 140 million non-U.S. users will be online. IDC Research found that 44 percent of users resided outside the United States in 1998. By 2002, the number is expected to rise to 58 percent. The Computer Industry Almanac estimates that by 2005, the United States will have 207 million registered users, but they will represent only 29 percent of the world total online.

Experts attribute the growth to several factors:

- More non-U.S. businesses want a piece of the worldwide market.
- Privatization and deregulation of telecommunications in many countries will continue to open the door to more service providers and help lower the cost of online access.
- Computer and modem sales continue to grow worldwide.
- Local Internet services are growing.

- Relaxed political control by national governments eases growth.
- The availability of greater bandwidth and improved technology facilitate growth.

It is clear from reading the results of various surveys and collecting anecdotal information that global markets are growing. According to Boston-based Information Gatekeepers, Mainland China's Internet market doubled to 1.175 million users in the first half of 1998. The New York City–based new media research firm, Jupiter Communications, reports that Germany is leading the way for European e-commerce. German business owners expected $1.8 billion in revenues from online sales of air travel, books, music, and software.

HOW LARGE IS THE WORLDWIDE MARKET?

Because the numbers issued by different market surveyors vary widely, it's difficult to quote definitive statistics. However, NUA Ltd., an Internet developer and research aggregator based in Dublin, Ireland and New York City, has compiled research from many sources to make an "educated guess." Here are the estimates as of September 1998:

Region	Number of Internet users
World Total	148 million
Africa	800,000
Asia/Pacific	22 million
Europe	22.25 million
Middle East	750,000
North America	87 million
South America	4.5 million

Reaching international customers will become a critical factor in one's success online. But not all the trends are up. Japan's economic problems seem to have carried over to its recent Internet activity. In 1998, reports Nikkei Multimedia in its Seventh Survey of Internet Active Users, the number of online shoppers in Japan actually declined slightly (to 46.6 percent of those surveyed, down from 48.3 percent).

While small businesses may have access to new markets around the world, global e-commerce requires more planning and preparation than merely putting up a Web site and waiting for orders to pour in. You'll need to investigate customs, tariff, tax, and distribution requirements and restrictions. The U.S. Department of Commerce is one source for the information you'll need. You should also consider consulting a qualified attorney.

A look at the Yahoo! Store may help us see how the lines in global commerce are becoming blurred. Some merchants report that they receive as many as half their orders from overseas customers. Although Yahoo! is a U.S.–based company, several of the businesses in its Store are based in other parts of the world.

A small manufacturer who had never sold direct, always relying on retailers to sell his products through their catalogs, decided the low cost of setting up a storefront on Yahoo! might open the door to selling direct. Just one day after posting the site, he received his first order. It was from the small Mediterranean island of Malta. After recovering from the shock and figuring out where Malta was and how to ship there, the order went out. Not only was the package received, but the customer expressed his pleasure by requesting status as the local Malta distributor. And that's how global relationships are born.

If you decide to test the global waters for your products and services, you will need to prepare yourself for this broader market:

Demonstrate your receptiveness to global business through your use of graphics, case studies, language options, and cultural awareness. If you have customers outside your country, be sure to include them on your site. Language presents a challenge because 1) you can't possibly include every language and dialect, and 2) you need to employ the services of a professional translator who can help you avoid embarrassing mistakes and misunderstandings. If you decide to translate all or parts of your site, select the languages spoken in countries your customers are most likely to come from—Latin America and parts of Europe and Asia, for example.

Make it clear up front that you welcome international orders. Nothing is more frustrating than finding a site that carries a product you want and are having difficulty locating locally, only to find when you try to place an order that the business (and Web site) is not set up to handle international e-commerce. If you are not yet ready to enter the world market, state this on your home page. If you plan to move gradually into the global arena, list the countries with which you currently do business. In short, keep your prospective customers informed.

Check your prices against those abroad. You may be surprised to find that even with the cost of shipping (assuming the items are not too large), you can beat the prices on many similar items sold in parts of Asia and Europe. The United States has greater manufacturing power, an abundance of skilled labor, available raw materials, and lower real estate costs. All these assets allow U.S. businesses to compete favorably with those in many other countries.

Use your Web site to establish your professionalism and build confidence in your business. Who do you feel more comfortable doing business with, the company closer to home that you know, or the company halfway around the world? If you are going to break down the natural inclination to buy locally, you need to win over your prospects. Sloppy presentation, misspellings, and a badly designed site will not win you any support, even if your prices are lower. Don't be perceived as a risk.

Know the law. I've said this before, but it's essential you know about any trade barriers or restrictions that exist. Don't wait until your first order comes in to learn whether or how you will fulfill it. If you have to go back

---

SIMPLIFYING THE GLOBAL DISTRIBUTION CHALLENGE

Using the Web as a distribution channel presents some interesting possibilities for global trade, because some products, especially in the music, software, information, and video areas, can be physically distributed across the Web. "This opens up tremendous benefits," notes Yahoo!'s Tim Koogle, for instant customer satisfaction and significant cost savings for business owners.

"There's a very interesting set of mechanics, evolutions, and steps that I see truly realigning the classic limitations of the physical sales channel and the physical distribution channel. It has to do with logistics. If you have software products that are amenable to distribution across the Internet, you have a worldwide market at your fingertips, without boundaries. And you don't have to deal with production of floppies, CD-ROMs, or other physical media. The business comes down to you. With your content, you only have to decide how to manage the transaction and secure it. That's tremendously powerful, and the market potential in our knowledge-based world is huge.

"I have no doubt that online distribution will continue to grow and encompass more and more examples of content, services, software, audio, music, video, and more. I also have no doubt that, managed well, there is real profit potential."

---

to the customer to say you can't complete the transaction, you will have lost your credibility as well as the sale.

HABITS OF ONLINE CONSUMERS

Let's test some of our theories about online shoppers and buyers against the published studies. NetSmart Research reports that among those interviewed (people in the United States who spend at least one hour a week online from home), these conclusions can be made. (Note that comments in parentheses are my own, offered to help you begin to put statistical findings to work.)

- *62 percent of consumers used online information to influence retail purchases.* (Even if you don't take orders online, your Web site can impact your offline sales.)

- *50 percent turn to the Web first for information.* (Don't make your Web site an afterthought; more and more people are looking to the Web first. Develop your Web site with an eye to building your brand and persuading a prospective customer to buy from you.)

WHAT ATTRACTS CUSTOMERS?

As part of an Ernst & Young study, online customers told researchers what they look for in an online business. The following responses are presented in the order of their importance to the consumer:

1. Well-designed and easy to use
2. Strong company brand
3. Sales of known, branded products
4. Alliances with popular search engines, portals, and communities
5. Aggressive advertising and promotion of the Web site
6. Evidence of being a fast follower
7. Strong executive leadership
8. More competitive pricing
9. Being the first to act

As online entrepreneurs, you should note with pleasure that having the lowest price on the Web and being the first to provide a particular service are not as critical as the reputation of the company, quality and brand recognition of its products, and the strength of the site design.

- *49 percent go looking for information without a particular brand in mind.* (The quality of your Web site and information about your products and services can turn a browser into a customer.)

- *93 percent use the Web to find specific information and select a brand when shopping for high-ticket items.* (This means your content is key, and so is your brand awareness. When a prospect selects your Web site based on past brand experience, don't disappoint.)

- *64 percent actually made their high-ticket item purchases based on online information.* (This is significant, and all the more reason not to underestimate the value of a strong, professional image.)

- *19 percent admit they go looking for entertainment and interaction when buying high-ticket items.* (This number is low enough, relative to the other numbers, to tell you that quality information, not audio and graphical bells and whistles, is what sells.)

- *83 percent will leave a site if frustrated with navigation.* (By all means, work hard to make your site intuitive and easy to navigate. Why bother to post information if it's hard to find?)

- *73 percent admit they will leave a site if it takes more than two or three clicks to find the information they are looking for.* (Online shoppers are typically in a hurry. Make shopping fast and convenient.)

- *Among online buyers, 81 percent paid by credit card. The number was slightly higher among those buyers with three or more years of experience online.* (With the tools and services available today, you can make your site reasonably secure for credit cards. Don't neglect your own protection. If you haven't yet signed up with a merchant program that verifies customer credit, the time to act is now.)

- *The average customer bought nine products and spent $475.* (While this number is higher than some others I've seen, it definitely supports the strength of e-commerce. We're not talking about small change.)

- *19 percent of online shoppers admitted to doing less traditional retail shopping, and 20 percent said they did less catalog shopping.* (E-commerce represents more than incremental sales. There is more and more evidence that online buying is replacing traditional shopping among an increasing number of consumers. Don't think catalogers are ignoring the trend. Apparel cataloger Lands' End reported a 17 percent decline in operating earnings during the fourth quarter of 1998. At the same time, its Web site booked $61 million is sales—more than three times its online sales in 1997. The company recently reported it was closing several retail outlets.)

In summary, we can see that branding matters for high-ticket items. Whether or not you sell on your site, you must build brand awareness. Content is critical for educating prospective buyers. For low-ticket items, price is most important. You will need to keep administrative costs low enough to make a profit. Those business owners with the lowest overhead and the most aggressive strategy will win sales in this category.

CATALOGERS GO ONLINE

While L.L. Bean, Levenger, Quill Corporation, Lands' End, REI, and Victoria's Secret are all watching their online sales rise, most (indeed more than half of the top 100 catalog businesses) have exercised extreme caution toward the Web. Recent numbers suggest that's all about to change. The fact is, online purchases are actually cutting into catalog sales.

It's easy to draw some basic similarities between catalog and Web-based businesses. Both have an edge over the brick-and-mortar retailer, for example, that must expand physically to expand its reach. It must hire more employees, pay more benefits, set up retail stores, expand operational systems and procedures, and rent warehouse space, all of which requires capital and can cut significantly into profits. Catalogers and Web-based business can expand their operations into new, larger markets without moving. But here the similarities begin to dissipate. Catalogers must print and mail catalogs, and even with price breaks associated with economies of scale, that can be expensive. Web entrepreneurs, however, only need to broaden their marketing and advertising reach. They have several other advantages over traditional retailers:

- Real-time merchandising: "Hot" items can become immediately available without the hindrance of long lead times, while out-of-stock merchandise can be removed from the site immediately.

- Unlimited pages make the cost of adding items negligible once the site is up and running.

- They are able to establish ongoing, interactive relationships with customers, including giving consumers a voice in deciding which products they want to see offered on the site.

- They can make more frequent product introductions, and products can be more easily tested, reading demand for an item in a matter of days or even hours without costly inventory commitments

- Pricing and promotion flexibility allow them to act quickly to spur sales of slow-moving merchandise. Sites can serve as "sales and liquidation" vehicles for catalogers to rid themselves of excess stock without disrupting their regular business.

- Visitors to the site who request catalogs or those who register there are strong leads; experienced online catalogers report that the conversion rate of "browsers" into shoppers is far higher than for names from rented lists. They also generally have higher income and other characteristics that make them particularly desirable shoppers.

- Incremental business can be generated by reaching customers who had not previously been exposed to the catalog.

- The newest personalization technologies can target customers one-on-one, offering them a totally customized product.

- Online catalog delivery can translate into a lower cost of doing business, especially as paper and postage costs continue to rise.

- Significant customer service cost savings can result from shifting catalog shoppers from telephone and mail order purchasing to online buying through the use of QuickShop and other electronic technologies.

1999—A WATERSHED YEAR

Based on the findings of Frank Gens, Senior Vice President of Internet Research, International Data Corporation expected 1999 to be the year that Internet use would become pervasive enough to reflect both the U.S. population at large and the world. Here is his list of key developments (if you want to review all of his predictions, go to www.idc.com/F/Ei/123199ei.htm):

- One-third of U.S. homes will be online; half will buy online (a significant market opportunity).

- Women will become the online majority in the United States. (If your products and services cater to women, you should begin trying to reach them online.)

- The United States will become an online minority. (Global opportunity will become a reality for businesses of all sizes.)

- Key IT markets will be shaped by the masses.

- Small businesses will flock to the Internet. (Will you be among them? If your business is not already online, this should be the year you stake out your territory.)

- Live phone support will become available in many Web stores. (This one of the recent trends in the integration of the Internet with other technologies. To make Internet shopping a one-stop experience, customers will increasingly be treated to real-time, voice-based customer service.)

- Web access will become available in many retail stores. (This reflects the increasing hybridization of retail. You can expect to see Internet kiosks in shopping malls and retail stores that have a strong Internet presence.)

- Financial realities will drive Internet stock corrections. (Much of the trading in Internet stocks has been based on expectations of profits to come. Many stockholders are going to start looking for real return on their investment. If you are considering taking your company public simply to cash in on the madness and win an infusion of capital, make certain your business plan supports your growth strategy. Otherwise, you may be disappointed.)

- Competitive realities will drive many Internet mergers. (Look for more and more mergers and acquisitions to be transacted. This is one way savvy business owners are gaining market stature. You may be the target of one of these acquisitions, or you may find the capital to buy someone else and strengthen your market position.)

AOL MEMBERS AS A MODEL

Although we have focused more on the state of the Internet, the proprietary service America Online (AOL) controls a significant portion of the marketplace. Its customers are increasingly using AOL as their portal to the Internet. You will need to factor the purchasing habits of AOL customers into your plans. If you visit the AOL Web site, you will find a wealth of buying trends.

- AOL membership matches the combined population of New York, Chicago, and Los Angeles.

- At 1.4 million, AOL International members represent the fastest-growing segment of the AOL market.

- AOL members increased their average usage by 16 percent during 1998.

- 23 percent of member time online is spent using e-mail.

- AOL members sent 34 million e-mail messages in 1998.

- Women account for more than half of AOL users, a significant increase since 1995.

- 58 percent of AOL households with children use Parental Controls.

- 57 percent of members of CompuServe, which is a subsidiary of AOL, have professional, executive, technical, or academic jobs.

- Co-marketing agreements and relationships continue to grow. During 1998, AOL consummated 50 commerce pacts worth more than $1 million.

- Trading in 1998 through AOL's Brokerage Center increased 321 percent over 1997.

- AOL's Shopping Channel is the number one shopping destination online. (Perhaps you should consider displaying your goods and services here.)

- 84 percent of AOL members have "window shopped," and 44 percent have bought goods online.

- More than 400 stores sell through AOL.

- Apparel, books, music, and computers were holiday best-sellers.

- AOL members purchased more than 1 million electronic greeting cards.

- More than 90 percent of the connections to AOL support 56K baud rates.

TIP

To help you keep current with the state of the Net, review the many free reports (others can be ordered for a fee) at the following sites:

Nielsen	www.nielsenmedia.com/interactive/index.html
Commerce Net	www.commerce.net
Jupiter Communications	www.jup.com
Nua	www.nua.ie/surveys/subscribe.html
eMarketer	www.e-land.com
Cyber Atlas	cyberatlas.internet.com
Cyber Dialogue and Find/SVP	etrg.findsvp.com

- AOL members account for more than 1 billion Web hits daily.

- AOL and CompuServe support 700 business and interest forums.

Although you can learn a great deal by studying your competitors' Internet practices, never lose sight of the fact that the key to success online is making the effort to develop an accurate picture of your own marketplace and the real opportunities it presents. That is what will enable you to identify the right strategies and tactics to achieve success online.

YOU DON'T NEED TO BE A TECHIE TO DESIGN A WEB SITE

You say you're not an artist. Neither are you a programmer. You have postponed designing your Web site because you lack the expertise. These are not valid excuses. In fact, your business and your Web site may actually benefit if you aren't too actively involved in the graphic and technical aspects of site design. As a business owner, your primary contribution should be strategic. The less time you spend playing with software, picking fonts, and selecting graphics, the more time you will have to focus on the bigger issues.

Without question, the more important challenges before you are to set objectives, organize information logically, define the ideal customer base, identify and create useful content, plan the marketing, and build strategic marketing relationships. "The biggest mistake business owners make, I believe, is to think of design only in terms of the graphics and programming of a Web site," explains Premiere Interactive's Jerry LoMonaco. "Even though I'm a graphic designer, I probably put fewer hours into the physical aspects of building a Web site than into helping my clients set objectives, understand how to achieve their objectives online, build relationships between the Web site and the rest of the business, and determine how all the pieces will work together to create a successful Web site."

NEED A WEB DESIGNER?

If you need a starting point to begin your search for a Web design firm, look to the Internet. If you find a site that you particularly like, look at the bottom of the home page for the name or logo of the company hired to design the site. If this does not yield a designer you feel comfortable employing, try searching the Web. Here are four services that can help you get started:

- Who Built It (www.whobuiltit.com)
- Ultimate Web Design List Yellow Pages (webdesignlist. internetlist.com)
- AAA Web Design List (www.aaadesignlist.com)
- Digital Talent (www.digitaltalent.com)

SET YOUR EXPECTATIONS AND DEVELOP A BUSINESS PLAN

Business owners considering how they will use the Internet in their businesses can start with three premises: "First, the Web is not going away," assures Mary Jeffries, Chief Operating Officer for Shandwick International, a communications firm. "You are going to have to deal with it. Second, you have to keep the site up to date if you want people to continue to visit. It can't be static. Once you decide to enter the Web market, you need to maintain and nurture your site. Third, don't expect hard data today to document what the Internet can do for you. There is not a lot available. No one can promise you X customers or X dollars in sales. That's why you must decide what it is you want to accomplish, then develop the most effective means to that end."

As you begin to develop the concept and content for your Web site, overlay these with your expectations and a realistic timetable for realizing them. In other words, develop a business plan. For example, in Year One, you might want to focus on building visibility for your online site. Perhaps you set a goal of 750 hits (visits to your site) and 80 good customer leads per month. "It's not so much that the number of hits is subjective but that the number of hits is relative," explains Mark Towler, Phase 2 Development's CEO. "A small, local retailer looking to expand a mail-order business might be very pleased with an additional 400 hits per month if that results in 40 new orders. On the flip side, a larger retailer with plans for major sales growth based on Internet initiatives may be disappointed in 40 incremental sales and 400 new contacts.

"The important thing is to go through the exercise of developing some success measurements that are appropriate for your business. Some of the dynamics that help our company develop success measurements for clients include:

- size of an average sale;
- amount of presale activity required to move customers through each stage of the selling process;
- amount of post-sale service required to support each sale; and
- value to the company of each qualified lead generated by other marketing campaigns.

"With this type of information in hand, a company can start to set some expectations of return on investment, based on the investment in their Internet initiatives."

Shandwick International's Mary Jeffries suggests conducting pre- and post-awareness surveys as one means of testing strategies and adjusting assumptions. With this information and data on the rate at which hits, leads, and revenue grew during the first year, companies can set new goals for Year Two, and so on.

By the same token, if business owners see that they are falling short of expectations—and assuming their expectations are reasonable—they will know they need to redirect their efforts. For example, a low hit rate may indicate a need to step up marketing efforts. Has the company included its Internet address on all its brochures, stationery, trucks, advertising, and direct mail materials?

If visitors fail to return to the site regularly, a company may need to rethink its online content. Is there enough useful information? Is the front end of the site burdened with too many slow-to-load graphics? Are Web managers adding to and changing content frequently enough?

If one's existing customers are not using the site, the company may have to evaluate its online customer service and help features. For example, can customers get expert advice more quickly and easily by picking up the telephone and calling the company? If so, the company may need to capture that same expertise online and make it available 24 hours a day. Similarly, if your retail location or printed catalog offers a wider range of products than your Web site, customers who have been to your store or ordered by catalog are not going to be impressed by the online offering. Make all your products and services available online, and if possible provide even more online.

In the end, how companies approach their business plans for the Web is critical. Management should start with a set of realistic expectations for success and the means to measure it. Just as in any traditional marketing, promotional, or direct mail effort, the more information you have on what works and what doesn't, the better equipped you will be to face competition. Given the more level playing field the Internet provides all businesses, price alone will not be a winning formula. A company's strength may lie in its ability to use the Web to better inform and better service customers and prospects than the competition. Know your competitive advantage.

WHAT MAKES A WEB SITE WORK?

Wirthlin Worldwide (www.wirthlin.com) interviewed 1,007 household users of the Internet and reported the following conclusions regarding what customers and visitors want—and increasingly demand—from a Web site:

- Useful information (45%)
- Easy to navigate (38%)
- Well-designed (28%)
- Loads quickly (17%)
- Timely information (7%)
- Fun things to do (6%)

Setting Objectives

Like market research, setting objectives is a task you will need to revisit throughout your Web site's development phase. After you are up and running, you will need to reevaluate your original goals and continue to fine-tune your site. From time to time, you will probably even redefine your objectives. "Once you begin, the task of creating a Web site is never merely an objective," says LoMonaco. "It's a journey." The best way to set objectives for your Web site is to think in terms of building a business plan or blueprint. In the process of defining your goals, you begin to identify resources, set capital requirements, and estimate the return on your investment.

If you are currently running an offline business, and planning to continue doing so in tandem with your online effort, you must also integrate your goals for your Web enterprise into your overall business and marketing objectives. In this way, not only will you be better prepared to allocate resources and capital to the task and set a marketing budget, but start to think about the parts of your business that can benefit most from the Web.

You'll also begin to have a clearer picture of the business' potential and what percentage of your total revenue can come from e-commerce.

If you approach the online and offline aspects of the business as one entity, you may ultimately find yourself redefining your whole business. For example, you may find the Web is better suited to achieving your goals than a conventional storefront or walk-in office. If Egghead Software's management can rethink its business model and decide to stake its future entirely on Egghead.com, it's not hard to believe that you too could reach a similar conclusion. But the only way to be sure is to clearly establish your objectives up front, and constantly measure the results.

On a second, perhaps larger, more holistic level, investing your time in setting goals and objectives will give you greater insight. When you can define the problem at hand, a solution is usually easier to see. And implementation of that solution begins to take on a life, and direction, of its own.

JAMES COANE ON WHAT IT TAKES TO SUCCEED

Business is changing so rapidly on the Internet, it's difficult to keep up with the players and the business entities. When we first interviewed James E. Coane, he was president and COO of Wayne, Pennsylvania–based N2K Inc. The business focused on the development of original content and its packaging for the Internet. At the time of this interview, N2K was busy applying its talents to the development of an online music store called Music Boulevard. Like most of the Internet pioneers in e-commerce, Music Boulevard experienced heavy losses during its start-up phase, but went public late in 1997 and raised almost $70 million on its IPO. On March 17, 1999, Music Boulevard and its primary competitor in online music retail, CDnow Inc., merged to create the new, larger N2K/CDnow.

In this extract from our interview, Mr. Coane, president and COO of the newly merged entity, clearly and eloquently expresses the necessity for Internet entrepreneurs to unleash their creativity on a perceived problem to be solved. Creativity, without adequate planning and commitment, he believes, will not be enough to generate success in the virtual world.

First, you have to have a vision and a business strategy that defines your goals. And it has to be a winner. This is really no different from doing business in the traditional world. A lot of money is invested in a lot of good ideas that never win because the strategy is flawed.

The second key ingredient is creativity, and a lot of it. The Internet is an environment driven by the perception of having the coolest thing out there. I'm not just referring to graphics, or colors, or even effects. In order to build appreciation and a following—which could be converted into paying customers—you and your Web site must be perceived as innovative, creative, and leading-edge. Finally, you have to have the resources and money to establish your creative differentiators in the hearts and minds of the market.

For some offline companies, it will be very difficult to make the transition. You can look at many well-established brands in the conventional marketplace and imagine how difficult their transition to the virtual world will be. These companies—and they're fine companies with valuable brand identities—are firmly rooted in the strategies that breed success in the conventional business arena. For this reason, I don't know how effectively a Sears or Kellogg or Post, to name a few traditional brands, which I single out here only for their recognition value, will be at translating their brand power into a virtual world. Ultimately, will they be the big winners in merchandising on the Internet? Or will it be the Internet start-ups that succeed?

I do know that we are coming at the market from a very different frame of reference and perspective. And we aren't carrying the baggage of success in the traditional world. I believe that the Web entrepreneur has an edge because we think about the application of technology and information very differently from traditional retailers. As music retailers, for example, we think about what drives the decision to buy very differently from a manager in a book or music store. We have a different way of approaching the customer and responding to the customer's wants and needs. We see the technology and the information as tools to drive a more informed buying decision. The consumer wants to make an informed decision based on the best possible content we can provide, displayed in a way that makes it easy to find and easy to use. I think we do that better than the tra-

ditional retail environment. If consumers are impulse-driven, our approach to design and integration of cool services should also appeal.

My advice is to be courageous. But you also have to do your homework, analyze your markets, understand customers' needs, and have a clear image of the problem you are trying to solve. Look at the Internet as a tool—a communications tool, a publishing tool—not as an environment that is the be-all and end-all. But be prepared to spend more money and time than you thought.

DESIGN YOUR SITE WITH PURPOSE

As you prepare to develop your Web site, expect at least 75 percent of the effort to be in the conceptual phase. After you assess your business strengths, identify your audience, develop goals, and set a strategy, you can begin to settle on a key message and set your expectations for return on your investment.

Only when you know what you want to do and why are you ready to decide how. The "how" is and will continue to be a moving target. "We used to recommend developing sites around a metaphor or theme," explains Shandwick's Mary Jeffries. "But the best sites no longer do that. It's already an old trend. The idea, for example, of using a visual of a receptionist as the entry point into a professional services firm has given way to more straightforward design, ease of use, and direct access to the information needed." While this doesn't mean a company can never use a metaphor to express a concept, particularly one that's highly complex or dry, it does illustrate the imperative to stay abreast of industry trends. The world moves fast on the Web.

"At the same time," adds Phase 2 Development's Mark Towler, "you want to separate yourself from the crowd by doing something your competition is not. Road kill is probably a severe term, but it represents what you are going to see with some companies if they can't understand how to develop a competitive advantage or secure their niche." Perhaps a marketer of business travel would use its Internet presence to discuss very practical and up-to-date dos and don'ts of international travel and customs. For example, when bringing a gift to a customer in another country, which gifts are appropriate? Which might offend? What color paper should be used to wrap the gift? This is a useful service that is not readily available.

ARE YOU READY TO BRING YOUR WEB PAGE ONLINE?

Several steps precede the actual development of a Web site. To determine how ready you are, give yourself 10 points for each question below to which you answer "yes." Add up your score and compare it with the analysis in "Your Readiness Quotient."

1. Have you fully assessed your business opportunities and expectations for the Internet? _____

2. Have you identified your audience and crafted a message that supports your objectives? _____

3. Do you have an Internet Service Provider (ISP)? There are more than 4,500 ISPs in North America alone, according to *Boardwatch,* the magazine for network administrators (http://www. boardwatch.com). MCI, AT&T (which now handles IBM's service), and MindSpring are among the largest providers, and they can offer a variety of value-added services and broad exposure. _____

4. Did you make a site plan on paper, indicating where graphics will be and how hyperlinks will function? _____

5. Have you explored the possibilities for enhancing your site by adding links to other sites? If yes, give yourself 10 points and remember to contact the other site owners, tell them of your intention, and ask about establishing reciprocal links from their sites to yours. _____

6. Do you have a design presentation strategy? Graphics and sound provide sensory stimulation that will attract people to your site. The state of the art in graphics and audio is changing rapidly. With each new set of tools, such as Sun Microsystem Inc.'s Java™ and Macromedia Inc.'s Shockwave™, the Web becomes more of a multimedia experience. But it's good use of all components—content, graphics, and sound—that makes a site successful. _____

YOUR READINESS QUOTIENT

Score   **Readiness**

60   Congratulations and good luck. You're ready to go live
               with your site.

40–50   You're almost there. Have you given enough thought to
               the ongoing marketing and promotion needed to make
               your site successful?

0–30   You still have a lot of preliminary work to do before going
               on the Internet.

- Step 1: Identify an ISP.
- Step 2: Identify and research your audience.
- Step 3: Locate and study your competition online.
- Step 4: Set your objectives and lay them out in a
  business plan.
- Step 5: List the components you want in your site.
- Step 6: Design the site.
- Step 7: Create your content.
- Step 8: Develop a plan for adding new content
  and keeping the site current.

Mary Jeffries offers another way to approach the challenge of market differentiation. "Focus on the information, not the selling," she says. "It's the soft-sell approach I call 'assisted interest.'" For example, if your site is an extension of your office furniture business and you specialize in ergonomic equipment, help your prospective customers select the right chair or other furniture. In other words, share your expertise. If the choice is dependent on one's height, or physical condition, then provide rules of thumb and advice that will guide the purchase. Or focus on some related benefit, such as suggested exercises someone can do at his or her desk to keep alert and avoid developing a repetitive stress injury. It's a soft sell that provides customers with valuable information that will help them come to the ultimate conclusion that they want to buy from you. When updated and appended regularly, such sites attract customers and prospects to visit regularly. Focus on creating a site that's clear, simple, and logical and reflects your objectives. By all means, build a site that has the capacity to grow with your goals.

Organize Logically for Greatest Impact

The very nature of an entrepreneur is to jump in and make things happen and worry about the organizational details later. Entrepreneurs act on their ideas and inspirations by applying 110 percent of their time and energy to their vision. While you may not usually approach business as a series of tasks to be organized, creating a successful Web-based business demands organization. A Web site is an entity you launch and, in a sense, turn over to a waiting audience. Like a book or magazine, you develop content for your Web site and publish it. Then it's hands off: You turn control over to your readers, customers, and prospects to use as they see fit.

If you watch people read a magazine or newspaper, you'll notice that very few do so in the same manner. Some people peruse a magazine starting at the back and working their way forward. Others study the table of contents and read selectively. *The New Yorker,* which offers readers a rich and varied fare, elicits all manner of reading preferences. Many go through and look at all the cartoons first. Others start with the calendar of events. Most people I know put off reading the feature stories until they can block out enough time to read them through in one sitting. When reading newspapers, most people start with the headlines, then quickly begin to move around to their favorite sections, looking for the information they expect to find. The content is different each day, but the categories of content remain fairly constant. There's the business section, sports, world news, and so on. Most readers have one or more favorite columnists, and often can't abide other columnists.

The point is that a Web site, like a magazine or newspaper, is not read in a linear, sequential fashion. We jump around to the sections we think will give us the most information or the greatest pleasure. As a Web designer, it's up to you to anticipate how people will view your Web site, then develop an environment that makes their job easiest. This is where organization comes into play. It may help you to visualize your Web site as a flowchart or map, draw it on paper, and then have it translated into Web pages.

Categorize and Compartmentalize

A Web site should not be a digital regurgitation of a brochure, catalog, or pamphlet. It may contain all the same material and messages, and at the same time include press releases, customer case studies, worksheets, company history, and more. But the information (we call it content) needs to be presented in short blocks or chunks. You're not creating a sequel to *Moby Dick* on the Web. You're creating an environment, almost a miniature world, that is rich in information and that your visitors will use for their edification and enjoyment.

As a businessperson, you hope to turn those visits into dollars, whether through the sale of goods and services or advertising and co-marketing relationships. Your Web site is an amalgam of textbook, picture book, computer program, television, advertising, catalog, convenience store, and so on. It will work only if visitors can find their way through the clutter. The more diverse the world you create, the more visitors will rely on you to dish it out in manageable chunks organized logically and intuitively. You want people to find what they're looking for quickly and have the option of digging as deeply into a subject as they want. This is where the "chunking" of information becomes critical. Someone who wants only a cursory description of several topics should be able to scan horizontally across all categories. When you find something of interest, you can move vertically, with each layer providing more in-depth and perhaps more technical information. Here are a few basic rules for categorizing and compartmentalizing your content:

- *Use an outline format for laying out information.* All information at the same horizontal level should have equal weight or importance. The chunks of information should all be about the same length. Subsections provide ever-increasing detail and specificity.

- *Text that is written primarily for online consumption should be brief.* No one enjoys reading streaming pages of text on a computer screen. If you want to include white papers or chapters from your book, allocate them to categories to be downloaded or printed for later reading.

- *Take full advantage of hypertext to link related chunks into a logical flow, both horizontally and vertically.* Try to anticipate the many ways readers may associate information: The browser may want a little top-level information on many topics, while the reader may want to study one topic in depth.

- *Create chunks of information that satisfy the expectations of both browsers and readers.* There is no magic formula for determining how long or short a chunk should be. The only measures you can apply are usefulness and functionality. Avoid long-winded, adjective-laden text. Get to the point, but be sure you do make a point.

Establish Hierarchy and Relationship

You can't really compartmentalize your content until you visualize a hierarchy for information. Think of the top level of your hierarchy as chapters, the Web map as the table of contents. Define the first layer of your hierarchy in terms of your site's functionality. If you are a public company, you'll have a section on investor information. You'll probably also want to give some background on your business, brief biographies of key employees, and lists and directions to the locations of your offices. Perhaps you see all this information as secondary to your business objectives. If so, you may want to lump investor information and corporate information together under "Operations" or create an "About Our Business" section.

Similarly, if yours is a fast-paced industry with new products, inventions, and developments requiring you to update your Web site daily or even hourly, you will probably want to make the "What's New" section prominent. In this case, the "What's New" section should also appear at the top of your hierarchy. This information needs to be refreshed regularly, and the older information incorporated into other categories or archived or both.

The products and services you offer fall into another prominent category. The specifics about each item will follow the vertical hierarchy you develop. For example, if you sell technology, consumer electronics, or anything that requires listings of benefits, examples, and technical specifications or usage requirements, each one of these subcategories should fall under the same horizontal level of your hierarchy. In other words, each product or service should be defined in the same logical order, and with horizontal and vertical linkages clearly delineated.

The point is that all the categories you create within each layer of your hierarchy should have the same relative weight. Put apples with apples and oranges with…well, you get the message. Your Web site should not spill out like a mixed basket of produce.

Here's an example that will better explain what I mean: You have a product line called ACME Whistle Stompers, which you manufacture in several configurations. Each configuration, or model, has its own specifications, is designed for a particular set of uses, and carries a different price. Your prospective buyers understand the basic application of the Whistle Stomper but need more information to determine which model is right for their business. In this case, they may not want to follow a vertical path through each description. They may want to cut to the bottom and just review the technical specifications for each model. Or perhaps they will want to read a series of application stories that describe each Whistle Stomper in real-world business situations. To help your prospect follow his or her personal preferences and logic, you must create the appropriate relationships.

Once you have established a hierarchy and have categorized your content within that organizational design, you can begin building relationships. There are several kinds of relationships or links you can establish. The horizontal and vertical relationships described already, are the easiest and most obvious. But sometimes you'll need to create links to very disparate elements. For example, you may indicate that for customers to make a selection, they need to analyze their needs first. If you have created a utility, an interactive tool, or even a matrix that helps customers calculate their requirements or identify their classification, you will need a link to this location. In this case, each product or service will link to the same tool.

Other links may require going outside of your Web site or bringing someone else's site into a window within the context of your site. For example, if you are a reseller or distributor for another company, and that company has created its own Web site rich in product information, you can rely on the manufacturer to provide detailed information you don't have or don't want to develop. Building such a relationship requires you to work out an agreement with the other company. Typically you won't have any problem setting up an intercompany relationship, and often you can negotiate a reciprocal link to your Web site. From a technical perspective, this type of link is called a "hot link."

TIP

Here's a word of warning about how to name your site's departments: "What's New" is precisely that. In offering this category, you are automatically setting your visitors' expectations. Don't post information to "What's New" and leave it there for several months.

HOT LINKS AND HYPERLINKS

In the interactive environment of the Internet, and specifically the Web, the ability to move quickly and seamlessly to in-depth or supporting information or related Web sites is one of the more powerful features at hand. By simply moving the cursor to an icon, an activated graphic, or a highlighted word or phrase and clicking the mouse button, Web users are instantly transported to the linked data or site. Linking to a related site outside of the current Web site is a hot link, and moving to a different location or layer within the same site is a hypertext link or hyperlink.

Finally, there is another type of relationship you will probably need to factor into your design. Think of it as "backup." If your industry tosses around a lot of technical jargon or tends to invent its own words, which is what happens in the computer field all the time, you may want to use the technical term, but provide a definition or explanation. In this case, you would link a word or phrase to a glossary section. When someone clicks on a hyperlinked word, a definition appears on the screen. Similarly, you may have cause to mention a person or product a viewer is not familiar with. Again, all you do is create a hypertext link to some backup information. You'll find that you apply these types of relationships very irregularly. There is no pattern or hierarchy to follow. They simply appear wherever in the text they are appropriate.

Let's review the various hierarchies and relationships graphically:

FIGURE 6-1 Your hierarchy will look relatively simple until you start adding the relationships. Then it begins to take on the look of a coach's chalkboard.

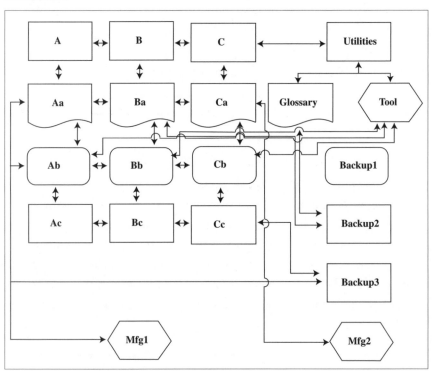

But Is It Functional?

Without leaving the subject of organization, let's jump ahead for a moment. Your Web site is all laid out. You have a hierarchy that is logical to you and, you hope, intuitive to your visitors. But is it? Does it really work? You can study your flowchart and use it as a blueprint to build your Web site, but only after you have laid out the pages and created a working model will you be able to test its functionality. The more people you ask to try out the site before going live, the better. This is why it is important to track how visitors use the site and invite their feedback. Note that if you are worried about infringing on users' privacy, tracking can be completely anonymous. You are not interested in who does what. You are interested in how all visitors navigate the site. You want to know, too, where they spend the most time.

Although it will take months, and probably several refinements, to make your site highly functional, here are some questions you should ask yourself during the development phase:

- *Will first-time visitors come into your site and find exactly what they are looking for?* Track their movements, ask for feedback, and even try to arrange to watch a first-time user look for information. Finally, make your site map and search engine prominent to help them.

- *Will they quickly find the information you want them to see up front?* Apply the same rule we use in writing: Don't bury your lead. Long, convoluted, and even too-clever copy can obscure your message, even when you place it on your site's home page.

- *Will they understand the logic behind your design (the hierarchy and relationships) and move toward their goal effortlessly?* If you don't get it right the first time, you won't be alone. Don't give up; keep fine-tuning your efforts.

- *Are all the basic categories accessible within one or two clicks of the mouse?* Faulty navigation can loose you a good prospect and make even an old customer look elsewhere.

TIP

Make it clear in a policy statement that all tracking is anonymous and is done for studying Web activity only.

- *Can visitors move horizontally through information as easily as they can move vertically?* Give them the option to read dynamically in their own fashion.

- *Does the flow of information lead prospective customers to a logical conclusion?* In other words, if you are selling pens, will they be able to make a selection from your inventory, feel comfortable that they have made the right choice, and move effortlessly to your order form?

- *Is it easy for visitors to back up and move in another direction?* You want to be able to throw your visitors a life preserver any time they need it. Give them a direct path back to your home page, the shopping cart, or any other major category. You'd be surprised how often this feature is missing. I've used sites at which one false move threw me out of my task and required me to log back on with my name and password before I could resume shopping.

- *When all else fails, do customers and prospects have an obvious alternative means to contact your firm, ask a question, or receive help?* Make your e-mail address, 800 number, and other information readily available and prominent. Don't lose a sale because someone wanted to talk with a company representative before ordering but couldn't find how to do that.

You can address the functionality of your design with a little thought and anticipation. There are several rules and functions you can build into your Web site that will help. The first is consistency of design and location. For example, post your primary categories (much the way a book includes a table of contents) at the top or along the side of every page. We'll call this a menu. When visitors move into a subcategory, you can expand the menu under the primary category to list each of the subcategories. This will aid browsers who have a propensity to jump around a lot, and it will help anyone get back to a home base.

A site map and a search engine are two additional tools to include. A site map can be a visual layout or a text-based outline of your site. It can look like a simplified version of your flowchart or an outline of categories and subcategories, and it serves much the same purpose as a book's index. Although it's ultimately up to you to decide how detailed you want it to be, just remember to make it functional.

Finally, so you can anticipate the free association many people prefer to make, supply a search engine that will 1) perform a text-based search of your entire site, and 2) list any matches in order of the strength of the match. In other words, if the search word appears in the title of an article or a dozen times in the first two paragraphs, the listing should appear before an article with only a casual reference to the topic of the search. It's a matter of applying a "measurement of confidence" that a particular article or other content will satisfy a user's needs.

TIP

One of the most frustrating experiences on any Web site is searching for the site map or search engine. All too many Web designers add these tools and then appear to go out of their way to hide them from the user. While they don't really hide them, when they forget to build them into the initial design the end result is often the same. These are valuable tools, not afterthoughts to be tucked in anywhere.

Factor Customer Service into Your Organization

Virtually all the elements we've mentioned serve the dual role of anticipating the way people will use your information and driving them to your ultimate objective—whether that's to pick up the phone and call you, visit the retail outlet closest to their home or office, or order goods and services directly from your Web site. Providing a high level of customer service is critical to your success online. For one thing, providing unparalleled customer service is an important way to drive activity to your Web site and away from your 800 number. If you can't afford to or don't want to provide 24-hour a day, 7-day a week telephone service, you can build this feature into your Web site.

One of the best features you can incorporate into your site is a section called "Frequently Asked Questions" or FAQs. This feature was spawned in the Web environment, and it is little more than a list of questions and answers that anticipates the most common problems and issues your customers and prospects face. Although you probably never called them FAQs, you have probably gone through a similar exercise in developing your brochure, fact sheets, direct mail flyers, or press releases.

On the Web, however, we give FAQs prominence. Some Web designers place their FAQs at the top level of their hierarchy. Others decide to locate this section under service or support. Wherever you decide to post your Frequently Asked Questions, make the section easy to find.

Once you've posted your FAQs, update them regularly. Keep track of the questions your customers ask when they come into your office, write or e-mail you, contact you by telephone, or send a fax. When you begin to see a pattern, post a new question and answer.

Finally, you can add to the value of your FAQs and direct more people to your Web site by referencing it in your voice mail message. When someone calls your office after hours with a question or request for technical help, don't simply tell them to call back between 9 a.m. and 5 p.m. Suggest they check out your Web site's FAQs. You may make many customers very happy. You may also be able to answer their purchasing questions and bring them to that critical decision—to buy—even when you and your staff are away from the office or unavailable. Finally, you can shorten the service and support queue that backs up on your phone lines.

Identify Your Ideal Customer

We've already addressed this subject in some detail in Chapter 5. Suffice it to say that you can't begin to develop content until you know whom you're trying to reach. Obviously you want to create a site that appeals to an audience with enough critical mass to support your enterprise. But what is unique about your audience? How do they use information? Do they expect to be entertained while they are learning about your company and its products? Are your prospective customers technically oriented? Or will they require you to spell out your products and services in very simple terms? Are you trying to attract the impulse buyer? Or are your prospects on a fact-finding mission? Online tire kickers will expect a greater depth of information than people who buy reactively.

The more you know about the composition of your customer and prospect base and the more accurately you can define their buying and shopping habits, the better you can create content that will appeal to your target market. Identifying your ideal customer is an important way to ensure the functionality of your Web site.

Create Content Designed to Work

Perhaps the biggest question on the minds of business owners new to the Web is "How do I make it work for me and my customers?" Because information is the most basic common denominator, business owners need to factor its dissemination into their online sales and marketing plans.

"It's not about networking your computers," explains Phase 2 Development's Mark Towler. "It's about leveraging your intellectual capital through the technology. Your business experience, your knowledge of your products and services and industry—these are every business owner's greatest assets. The task then is to 1) align this networked world with your business objectives, and 2) use technology and content to leverage your human intelligence through collaboration and information sharing in order to compress your product-to-market-to-order cycles. It's about generating leads and selling through your ability to provide the right content, customer service, technical support, and quick order processing."

Entrepreneurs serving the business-to-business market will find the focus on information to be a natural extension of their current sales process. If this is your market, you are probably in the habit of spending time talking with prospective customers, helping them understand the many ways your business can serve them, and even guiding them through the selection and purchasing process. When your business performs work for hire or manufactures to a customer's specific requirements, you have to walk them through many steps, anticipate their questions, and estimate costs and time of delivery or completion of the contract.

To serve the many requirements of customers, you typically create brochures, fact sheets, price sheets, and schedules, all designed to educate and inform them and help you close the business expeditiously. The same thought and care goes into designing a functional Web site. Create the content that will serve the needs of your customer and earn you the business.

In the traditional world of retail, catering to the needs of customers can be somewhat different. Although business owners must inform their prospective customers (shoppers) and help them make the transition to becoming buyers, their techniques may be less obvious at first glance. For example, when people shop at a large discount store, they are typically looking for a wide selection and low prices. Most expect to sacrifice some degree of sales help in exchange for a good deal. But they need information from someone, somewhere. That information may come from a television, print, or radio advertisement; a flyer received in the mail; a testimonial from a friend or colleague; an infomercial; a trade show or showroom display; or even the product packaging.

Everyone relies on some form of information to reach a purchasing decision. Even the impulse purchase—something picked up and handled at the register during checkout—requires some form of educational or promotional pull. If you only look at the product while a checkout person rings up your order, that can provide sufficient opportunity to formulate a decision to buy or not.

On the Web, the word *content* is used to describe information, interactive tools and worksheets, FAQs, technical specifications, graphics, discussion forums, and archived information—virtually anything you post on your Web site. The challenge is to present that content in a fashion that appeals to customers and prospects alike and to display it in a way that makes it both compelling and easily accessible.

How you create your content depends on several things, including the age of your business, how well-known you and your products are (via branding), the many ways you have reached customers in the past, your creativity, and how much money you have to spend. Entrepreneurs who have been conducting a similar business offline and are now making the logical leap to the Web have an advantage. They have already formulated many of their messages. They may even have printed up brochures and other materials in the past, much of which can be re-purposed for use on the Internet. The real advantages here are that, first, you can probably get your site up and running more quickly if you have information upon which to build. Second, you can save money because you won't be creating from scratch. But to be effective, the information must truly be re-purposed, not simply regurgitated. An electronic version of your brochure, for example, will probably have very little impact online.

By the same token, those with existing businesses face the challenge of ignoring many of the old tried-and-true ways. The Internet, by its very nature, requires each of us to think outside the box. This is the challenge James Coane referred to earlier in this chapter, and it can be the hardest task you'll ever face. It's in our nature, at the very core of our being, to cling to what's worked in the past. For this reason, we all tend to create associations (even artificial ones) between the old and the new. It makes life seem more comfortable, more manageable. But for a business moving onto the Web, it can also spell disaster and almost certain failure.

If you are a start-up, you face a different set of challenges. You will have to take the time to develop your messages. These will then need to be translated into formats that work online. If you are a bootstrap operation, you'll probably find yourself having to create much of this content yourself. Otherwise, you'll need to hire writers or a creative team to develop content for you. There are, however, a few tricks you can employ to help keep costs in line:

- *If you resell or distribute another company's products,* look to the manufacturer to provide you with some useful content. They may have testimonials, case studies, and technical information you can use. As I suggested earlier, you can even form online relationships and add reciprocal links between your Web site and other sites. This will give all parties more exposure (improving your chances of being found) and allow you to leverage each other's content. Why reinvent the wheel?

- *You can offload some of the work by providing a discussion forum or posting customer comments.* The people who use your products and services are often your best references. Let word-of-mouth help you sell. The discussions that take shape online are interesting, and the content that accrues is free.

- *Don't try to be all-inclusive your first day online.* Trying to deliver every conceivable piece of content up front is counterproductive. It makes it harder for you to come up with new information, the fresh content that helps keep people coming back for more. At the same time, plan for eventual complete content.

- *Remember that sometimes a picture really is worth 1,000 words.* Charts and tables can say as much as a short essay. A graphical presentation is often easier and faster to digest. You may just make the buying decision more convenient for your prospective customers if you provide visuals.

- *Post copy sparingly.* Don't go on for pages and pages (or in this case, screens and screens). Keep your messages short and to the point.

- *Present content in many different formats.* Posting a Q and A or transcribing part of a speech or interview is a welcome break from prose. You may also find it an easier way to write yourself. If you don't already have a speech or a press release you can re-purpose, try talking into a tape recorder. Then transcribe the tape and edit what you said.

One final design consideration that may help make the development and management of content easier and more cost-efficient is the use of a template and database. If you expect to be posting large amounts of content on your site, and if the information has a long shelf life and should remain available to visitors for months or years, you can simplify the data entry process and save on graphic designer fees by storing text and graphics in a database. Each file is linked to a template. When a visitor clicks on a choice from a menu or submenu, the system refers to the database, selects the appropriate copy and any linked graphics and charts, and downloads them into a predefined template.

For example, if you have a large number of archived case studies, a visitor to your site can read any of the stories just by selecting a title. The article appears on the screen in a format that will be the same for every case study. The text changes, and the graphics if you so decide, but the general format remains the same. With this type of design, it is easy and inexpensive for members of your staff to update content and add new information.

Oversee the Technical Decisions

It's time to put the many elements I've mentioned together and build a Web site. I said at the beginning of this chapter that to create a Web site you do not have to master HTML (the programming language used to create Web pages), have a degree in graphic design, or try to master one of the many design tools on the market. I went even further to suggest that focusing on the page layout, graphics, and technical aspects of Web design could actually hurt your business, because these tasks will take you away from the more important work related to the conception and organization of your Web site.

That said, having a passing acquaintance with some of the strengths and limitations of the Web will help you. For example, you need to understand that how people access the Web, what kinds of computers they use, and the sizes of graphic files are important to Web design. You need to understand enough about the process of building and hosting a site to identify and interview Internet Service Providers. If you decide to host your site at your office, you'll need help setting up the system. You want to do everything possible to make your Web site run smoothly and accurately. Remember, the more your site is "down" (not accessible) and the longer it takes for visitors to see and use your site, the more likely you are to frustrate potential customers and lose business.

The more you understand the stages of successful Web development and deployment, the easier it will be for you to understand the issues involved in costing out your site. Subsequently, this information will allow you to keep your costs to a minimum. You should be aware of:

WHAT'S IN A NAME?

To register a domain name, contact Network Solutions Inc. (InterNIC) directly or ask your Internet Service Provider to handle the registration process for you for an extra fee. Go to the Web site (www.networksolutions.com) to check for domain name availability, then fill out the registration form. The process takes about two days and requires an annual fee of $35 (for all sites registered after April 1, 1998).

Be aware of trademark issues. Although InterNIC does not check into trademark infringement issues, you are reminded to verify that you are not infringing on a federally registered trademark. Electronic addresses are not currently addressed by trademark law, and most lawyers believe it will take years to resolve this issue. For now, you might want to consult an attorney who specializes in intellectual property to conduct a trademark search. This usually costs between $100 and $300; trademark registration will cost another $700 to $1,000.

Note that Network Solutions' contract to offer exclusive registration services for domain names in the United States has ended. You can expect greater competition among services in the future.

- What the costs are and why they are necessary;

- What help you can expect from your ISP in keeping your costs down;

- What outside expertise you will require.

Beware of the firm that quotes you a fixed price for a Web site before fully understanding your objectives. That firm is not doing justice to you or to the Internet's capacity to solve your business and marketing requirements. Quoting a fixed price for a Web site is equivalent to an advertiser saying it will place your ad for $500 without knowing which of their magazines or newspapers you want to appear in, the size and color of your ad, how long your ad will run, or who is going to design your ad. (If you want the advertiser to design the ad, they will probably charge an additional fee.)

The Medium Really Is the Message

The similarities between print and online media are obvious. Both, for example, rely heavily on text and graphics. Both serve as sales and marketing tools. Both either promote a product or build brand and image awareness. It's the differences that are critical, however, and you must learn to exploit those differences.

Knowing that Web users are likely to expect a certain level of information before doing business online, many companies try to give users what they want by posting their brochures and other promotional materials on their Web sites. In theory, this is not a bad first step. The flaw typically lies with the execution. Rather than adapt (re-purpose) their brochures to the online medium, many are content to scan their brochures into a format for the Web and post page after page of text. But anyone who has spent much time online knows that viewing long screens of text quickly bores readers. The medium is not conducive to large blocks of copy. This is an environment made for visuals, sound, movement, and short blasts of text.

By the same token, if the content does not live up to expectations, all the images and color in the world will not make up the shortfall. Like the best print collateral material, the best Web sites effectively meld graphics *and* content.

Using graphics. Translating the audiovisual experience to the Internet requires an understanding of the current state of the technology. While it has come a long way in a short time—with sound and animation becoming easier to develop and simpler for users to enjoy—many users still view Web sites at 14.4 or 28.8 baud rates (the unit for measuring the speed of data transmission). Even though the newer modems transfer data at a rate of 56.6 baud, many service providers cannot yet support the increased speeds; and ISDN, DSL, and cable connections are not available everywhere. Large, full-color graphics load slowly, even at higher speeds, and waiting for graphics to appear can be as big a turn-off as trying to read page after page of streaming text. Until the average viewer has fast access, business owners should design their sites with these functional limitations in mind.

This does not mean, however, that you have to completely abandon color, animation, sound, and great graphics. Rather, it requires finding the right balance between compelling screen images and load time. Try using lower resolutions (90 DPI or dots per inch is adequate). Convert graphics to .GIF and .JPEG formats, which result in smaller file sizes. If you want to add special effects and larger images, give visitors options for viewing or listening. For example, postage-stamp size images allow users to see small versions of the graphics and choose to enlarge only the ones of interest. As a general rule, images larger than 50,000 bytes (50K) will slow loading and drive away many potential customers who use slow modems. Adhere to the old adage that less is more to create a visually appealing site that is clean, a pleasure to read, mentally stimulating, and easy to navigate.

Applying hyperlinks. Companies would probably have to go a long way to provide too much information on a Web site. The skill is in putting readers in control of how much information they want to read. By breaking text into discrete chunks and tying them together in a logical fashion using hyperlinks, you allow visitors to delve as deeply as they wish into certain topics and skim the surface of others. Hypertext links are the highlighted words (represented in a different color and often underlined) that are linked to other blocks of text. Click on a hyperlink word, and you are automatically transported to the related information.

Think of a hyperlink as a way of nesting information or creating an outline, with increasingly detailed information or related subject matter available as one moves from hyperlink to hyperlink. Effective use of hyperlinks puts visitors in control of how they use your Web site. They can get as much or as little information as they want. Hyperlinks can also be used with graphics.

Adding interactivity.   One of the great contributions to communications the Internet offers is the opportunity for the two-way transmission of information. The Net is not a passive medium. Involving visitors through the use of tools that calculate, test, analyze, and assess everything from mortgage rates and retirement nest eggs to the best car for a family of four gets visitors involved, helps them make decisions, and provides an environment for performing "what if" scenarios. Also try online forms that invite visitors to sign up for free samples, monthly electronic newsletters, or personalized information, and you have a legitimate reason to capture information about prospective customers that will build your database and help you learn more about customer wants and needs.

You can engage visitors with games, brainteasers, and access to special "members only" online resources. Or ask for their addresses and give them responses and information tailored to their geographic locations. With some simple programming, it's possible to collect data about visitors without infringing on their privacy. For example, it might be useful to monitor readership: What information is read? How long do people typically stay engaged? How many people visit the site each day, and how frequently do they return? You don't need names and addresses to collect these statistics. The Internet is a dynamic medium, and feedback can be used to change a site to meet ongoing interests and demand.

Inviting collaboration.   In many of the personal Web sites and an increasing number of business sites visitors are invited to enrich the existing content with their own experiences and knowledge. If it's appropriate, extend this option to your customers and prospects. Take the lead from the restaurant review and recipe collection sites that invite visitors to share opinions and add information. Not only does this encourage visitors to become participants, it helps keep your site dynamic. In business-to-business environments, companies have the added advantage of attracting a knowledgeable, professional audience. Their contributions will enrich a Web site for everyone's benefit. At the same time, some of the burden of adding new content is off your staff. Changing your Web site is key if you want people to keep coming back.

Shandwick's Mary Jeffries suggests thinking of a Web site as an event. Create an editorial calendar and stick to it. Change the site by event or season. Keep it modular. Have a clear idea of why you want to be on the Web. Don't be there simply because the competition is there. Be there because you understand the business advantages and are prepared to satisfy the online needs of customers and prospects.

PUTTING IT ALL TOGETHER TO CONTROL YOUR MESSAGE

Manufacturers and distributors have a vested interest in educating their customers about the features and benefits of their products. Business owners can apply this thinking to their Web sites, treating them as a form of online infomercial. Here they can deliver their message (e.g., public statements, press releases, customer testimonials, case studies, industry perspectives) undiluted and in a format that best serves the business objective.

Now, let's apply some of these techniques to a hypothetical Web site. Here's my interpretation of a site that promotes a new product, collects information, stays current, and serves as my personal Internet infomercial:

My company has developed a new brand of audiotape that is very thin and very strong and enables customers to buy recordable microcassettes that run for ten hours (five hours on each side). The sound quality is superb, but the price, at least initially, is on the high side, to help recover my research and development costs. I want to extol the benefits of my new tape and at the same time, test some prices before trying to sell local and national retailers on its merits.

I set up my hypothetical Web site to speak to my audience, which I believe falls into three categories:

1. *Teens* want to record all their favorite music and carry it with them for playing in the car or on a personal, portable tape player, without having to carry a backpack full of tapes.

2. *Journalists* conduct long interviews and require quality recordings good enough for playing as audio clips.

3. *Classical and jazz music buffs* have a number of old LPs they would like to record onto tape so they can listen to the music without wearing out their irreplaceable records.

I imagine there is also an application for tape backup of computer data, but I've decided to explore that later.

My hypothetical Web site includes the following:

- Promotion of my tagline, "Hours of Sound."

- Promotion for the tape's use in interviewing. I have recorded interviews conducted with famous people (entertainers, politicians, sports superstars, renowned journalists, and educators). I change these once a month to encourage people to keep coming back to my site.

- Spec sheets and comparison charts, including comparisons with the current competition, all designed to explain my tape's benefits quickly and clearly.

- An online demonstration of the sound quality. I record voice and music under a variety of conditions, which visitors to the Web site can hear if they are interested. To demonstrate the finer points, I include a wave chart comparing the highs, lows, base tones, and other indicators that would impress audiophiles. This also helps me overcome the sound quality limitations of many computers.

STRATEGIES FROM SOME OF THE BEST

In August 1998, Crain Communications' *Business Marketing* magazine released its NetMarketing 200, its editors' picks for the top 200 Web sites. Their primary criterion for selection was how effectively the site supported the company's objectives by providing a rich and rewarding online experience for customers and prospects. Although these are all large companies, you may gather some tips and techniques by studying their sites. Here are the companies and Web addresses chosen the top ten sites. (You can view the entire list by going to www.netb2b.com/nm200.)

- Marshall Industries (www.marshall.com)
- Cisco Systems (www.cisco.com)
- Bay Networks (www.baynetworks.com)
- Dell Computer Corporation (www.dell.com)
- Compaq Computer Corporation (www.compaq.com)
- Federal Express Corporation (www.fedex.com)
- IBM Corporation (www.ibm.com)
- W.W. Grainger (www.grainger.com)
- 3Com Corporation (www.3com.com)
- First Union Corporation (www.firstunion.com)

A follow-up study based on the top 50 sites on the NetMarketing list sheds some light on what these companies are doing right:

- 96 percent provide customer service and support online.
- 86 percent distribute their products via the Internet.
- 76 percent recruit employees online.
- 66 percent conduct e-commerce (take orders and payments online).

- Endorsements from top disk jockeys who have been using a commercial version of my product for the past six months.

- Hypertext links to technical data for those who want more detail. This is state-of-the-art audiotape, and there is a lot of technical information.

- A special offer to buy two tapes and receive a third (prerecorded by permission with ten hours of classical, jazz, or rock selections). I set the price at $50 and allow customers to request which type of music they want.

- Several pricing structures to test the market. For example, I sell the tapes individually ($25 each) and in packs of five (for $95).

- A secure, online order form to make it safe and easy for people to buy my tape. I include an independent certification of the security measures my site uses, as described by the developer.

- Press releases and press mentions I've received. As awareness for my product grows and my public relations efforts pay off, I'll update this section.

- An online discussion forum that encourages my customers to report their experiences, their thoughts about the product, and the many ways they are finding to use the tape.

CHALLENGE: CREATE A WEB PLAN

Here is another worksheet designed to help you document your objectives. While it shares some of the elements of earlier worksheets, this one is designed to free up your creative spirit. Let your ideas flow and capture them on the worksheet. Later, you can come back and fill in the details.

FIGURE 6-2 Here is a sample worksheet that lists everything I would like to incorporate into my Web site. Don't worry about the order in which you list items in the "Site Wish List" column. After you've listed all your ideas, you can go back and assign priorities and schedule their development and implementation. When you've studied the sample, try creating your own plan.

Site Wish List	Order of Development	Set Goals You Want to Accomplish	Content/Feature Type
Company Overview —Description —Services —Products	1st (2nd quarter 1998)	Explain our purpose, products, and services in a succinct and compelling fashion.	Text and graphics Bullet points
Staff-written articles	2nd (2nd quarter 1998) Add to this monthly.	Demonstrate our company's expertise with useful information.	Educational in nature, brief enough to be read online, searchable
Frequently Asked Questions FAQ)	3rd (2nd quarter 1998)	Anticipate customer and prospect needs by providing the information asked for most often.	Select the question and hyperlink to the company response. This should have drill-down capability.
Catalog	5th (3rd quarter 1998)	Print fewer catalogs and allow customers to order directly.	Graphical catalog that looks like the print version
Employee listings (with contact information)	4th (2nd quarter 1998)	Make it easy for customers to contact us.	Listing plus links to statements by employees
Interactive Tool	6th (4th quarter 1998)	Engage customers and prospects with a tool that helps them build their business.	Creativity generator that helps people exercise their business creativity

Finally, before you or your designer build the site, try laying out the elements outlined in Figure 6-2 in a flowchart. This will help you see how the elements relate.

FIGURE 6-3 Any number of software tools on the market can help you design a Web site flowchart. The more detail you include, the more clearly your designer will understand what you are trying to accomplish.

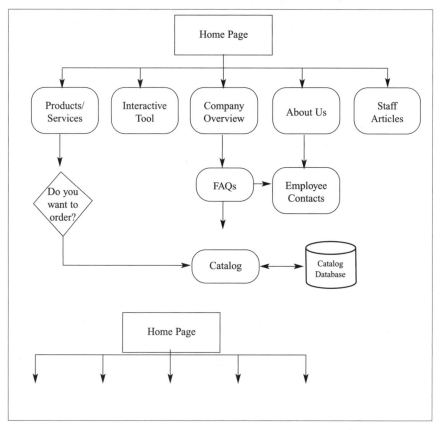

A NEW TOOL HELPS KEEP EXPENSES LOW

IBM has devoted considerable effort to the development of tools designed to facilitate Internet use for companies of all sizes. At the high end, IBM provides e-business consulting services, software tools rich in features and functions, a pantheon of security strategies, and outsourcing capabilities. IBM has selected from among these tools and services to create IBM

HomePage Creator for e-business (www.ibm.com/hpc), a resource scaled specifically for small, growing companies. IBM first introduced this online service in October 1997. Its initial success—as well as advancements in technology, increased demand from customers, and a growing understanding of what the owners of small and medium businesses require—has led to the introduction of a new, more powerful version of the original service.

Lee Warren, the developer of IBM HomePage Creator for e-business, created the service specifically with the small business owner in mind. "The template format and the way we step customers through each phase of design, development, and deployment have been conceived to alleviate the technical and artistic issues related to Web site design," he says. "I truly believe that business owners should concentrate on their business, what they need to tell customers, and how they say it. With IBM HomePage Creator for e-business, this is exactly what they can do. And the end result will be a clean, well-formatted site. The graphics will all be very professional.

"Furthermore, by integrating the tools and services required for e-commerce, business owners can post their sites in a matter of hours (not including the time they spend on the strategic issues) and get right to business. Finally, in an effort to provide our customers with the greatest flexibility, HomePage Creator for e-business will even support a Web site developed in HTML without the aid of our predefined templates. This makes our service a versatile and cost-effective choice for many business owners."

Business owners like it because the service is scaled to their needs today, and can be expanded as they grow. For a monthly fee starting at $24.95 for the basic service (five Web pages and a catalog of 12 items), to $200 (50 Web pages and 500 catalog items), business owners can quickly design Web sites that promote their business, showcase products and services, and provide the e-commerce functions needed to consummate financial transactions online.

In developing IBM HomePage Creator for e-business, IBM has helped reduce the physical and technical effort that goes into creating a site by providing a full-service solution that enables virtually anyone to build a Web site in a matter of hours. Using a point-and-click interface that includes galleries of hundreds of ready-to-use, professionally designed art and templates, customers are able to focus most of their attention on developing the content—the messages that best position their products and services.

In addition to design and content development, IBM HomePage Creator for e-business links to a full range of commerce and marketing tools. Among the leading services included are:

- *Site registration:* You have the option of using an extension of the IBM HomePage Creator for e-business Web address (mypage.ihost.com/yourcompany); or you can register a custom address (www.your company.com) through Network Solutions Inc. InterNIC for the standard, annual fee.

- *Search engine registration through LinkExchange's Submit It!:* At no additional cost, your site is listed with more than 20 leading search engine services.

TIPS FOR SAVING MONEY ON WEB DEVELOPMENT

- Employ a service, such as IBM HomePage Creator for e-business, with easy-to-use design templates and services ranging from Web hosting and catalog pages to online shopping cart facilities and secure credit card management.

- Purchase one of the Web site development tools, such as Microsoft® FrontPage 98, Adobe PageMill, or Corel WebMaster Suite.

- Hire a technologically adept marketer who has the interest and energy to learn about the technology and focus on it daily.

- Have your site hosted by an established Internet Service Provider and avoid the cost of buying a Web server as well as software and maintenance costs.

- *Secure online processing of credit card transactions:* Orders and credit card numbers are transmitted to Automated Transaction Services Inc. (ATS) where they are verified and safely stored. If you don't have a merchant account, ATS can help you establish an account.

- *Hassle-free Web hosting:* Your Web site is hosted on an IBM RS/6000® in a security-rich IBM facility with multiple T-1 lines connected to the Internet. You save on the costs of hardware, software, and maintenance.

Businesses of all types have benefited from the simple power and full-service capabilities of IBM HomePage Creator for e-business. For a single, low monthly expense, these businesses are enjoying online exposure and e-commerce. Couple the usage of this powerful service with a thorough understanding of your business objectives, a design that reflects those decisions, and the right mix of marketing and relationship building, and even a very small operation can grow quickly.

BUSINESS CASES FOR HOMEPAGE CREATOR FOR E-BUSINESS

Beyond the obvious advantages of using a product like IBM HomePage Creator for e-business—ease of use, low cost, and high functionality—is one that justifies anyone's exploring the possibilities. Quite simply, it's the fact that the speed with which you can create your site and the money you will save free you to focus your time and money on the single most overlooked aspect of Web development: marketing.

Small companies typically are neither as comfortable with nor financially able to spend aggressively on their marketing. As a result, they concentrate on their local markets. But with a tool like the Internet opening the doors to nationwide and global commerce, successful companies will need to invest more heavily in their promotion. The Internet is a double-edged sword: While it opens new markets, it also enables a company to get lost among the many businesses vying for opportunity.

I include here just three of the many case studies I have found of businesses and individuals using IBM HomePage Creator for e-business. They will serve, I hope, to reassure you that there is room for the small business on the Internet, and real potential to build your business beyond its current boundaries.

Business Case: Heritage Bed & Breakfast Registry (www.heritageregistry.com)
FIGURE 7-1

Objective: Bill Edlebeck began his bed and breakfast registration service in Chicago about ten years ago as a part-time hobby. After years of slow growth, the service had caught on enough to warrant taking office space and hiring one part-time employee. But the longer Bill ran the business, the more he wanted to see it grow.

Solution: Edlebeck decided to take his service to the Internet early in 1998. Here he can list Chicago bed and breakfast inns, describe their locations and ambiance, take reservations online, and remind guests about the full concierge services he provides. Guests can call his office to reserve a car, book theater tickets, and get recommendations on restaurants and local events. The results have been impressive. The business has grown virtually overnight. Whereas 60 percent of the business used to come through the city's convention and visitors' bureau, Bill now estimates that 80 percent of his business comes through the Internet.

Benefit: Listings change frequently, so Edlebeck needed a Web site that would be easy and inexpensive to update. He found that with IBM Home-Page Creator for e-business, he was able to build the initial site and register it with the major search engines in a little more than five hours. The success of the site has enabled him to expand the business, sign up new hosts, and build the kind of service that was once only a dream.

Business Case: Fess Parker Winery (www.fessparker.com)

FIGURE 7-2

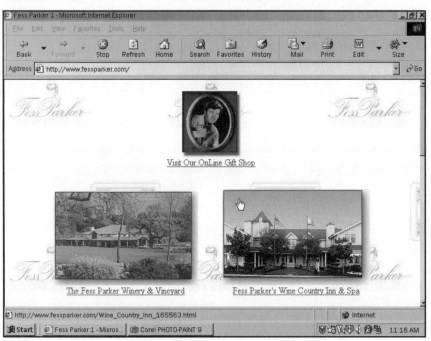

Objective: The difficulty for the new player in an established industry is getting recognition, building a customer base, and expanding distribution. In a few short years, the Fess Parker Winery, located in Santa Barbara County, California and owned by actor Fess Parker (of Davey Crockett fame) and his family, has made a name for itself in California, but national recognition has been slower to come.

Solution: Develop a Web site that promotes the winery, helps expand the wine club, promotes restaurants that serve Fess Parker wines, and makes it easy for followers of the wine to order direct from the winery 24 hours a day.

Benefit: Fess Parker Winery's existing customers are better served, new customers are found, and restaurants and hotels are encouraged to stock the wine in exchange for the extra publicity they receive through the Web site. By delivering an online newsletter describing wine events, festivals, new restaurants, and more, the winery encourages customers and prospects to return to the site regularly.

Using IBM HomePage Creator™ for e-business, Charlie Kears, general manager of the winery, has been able to develop a cost-effective solution that is helping to put the winery on the map. "I spend an hour or so each day working on the site, enhancing it, responding to e-mail, and adding new features," explains Kears. "Developing the site has been enjoyable and has certainly broadened our exposure. The wine club has more than doubled in size—to 8,000 members—in the year and a half we've been online." In the past seven years, the winery's annual production has grown from 4,000 cases to more than 35,000 cases marketed nationally, some of which can be attributed to online promotion and e-commerce (with shipping available to states where it is legal).

7

PLAN YOUR MARKETING AND BUILD RELATIONSHIPS

When your site is fully conceived, your work is still far from complete. For a Web site to survive and even thrive requires regular attention. As I've indicated before, Web sites need to be updated regularly and on schedule. A site is not a static thing to be posted and ignored. You can't sit back and wait for the orders to roll in month after month, year after year. An article in the November 1998 issue of *Business 2.0* suggests that the average life span of a Web page is 77 days. Many experts and business owners report that they add to and change elements of their content daily. You'll need to allocate some of your budget (both in dollars and time) to your Web site; if you ignore it, the opportunity lost could be priceless.

Marketing and relationship building are related to the issue of maintaining the Web site, but they should appear in your budget as separate line items. These tasks are critical to your business success. Even the best conceived site is worthless if no one knows it exists or where to find it. Promotion (or marketing) can be performed on a shoestring, if that's all your initial budget allows. But for broad impact, you will need to explore advertising opportunities, the creation of reciprocal links, and the development of relationships.

In the traditional world of business, we tend to limit our relationships to our suppliers, vendors, and customers. We typically do not cast far afield of our business or industry looking for companies with which to forge co-marketing relationships or referrals. Particularly, we do not think of aligning our businesses with traditional competitors. But as you probably are beginning to realize, the Web is a radically new medium. Customers hold the keys to your success, in part because it so easy for them to find another business online that will meet their needs. Satisfying customers—by creating value and convenience in many different ways—is your strategic objective. If satisfying customers means putting them in touch with a local vendor or distributor that can service their immediate needs in ways you cannot, then you need to forge the necessary relationships.

Similarly, building relationships that give you access to content and services you might not otherwise provide is equally important. Part of the convenience factor can be measured in terms of how fully, quickly, and cost-efficiently your site can serve the customer. To express this idea in more traditional, familiar terms, think of it as one-stop shopping. The more tasks a customer can complete in one location, the more convenient your Web site will be.

The range of marketing tactics you can employ and the number of relationships you can build are truly limitless. Because your most formidable competition adds to its war chest of tactics regularly, you need to do the same...or be prepared to be left behind.

Promoting and building your site are such critical and time-consuming tasks that you will need to budget your time carefully. Savvy marketing professionals allocate their time according to the Rule of Thirds: one-third to designing and posting the site, one-third to marketing and attracting prospective customers, and one-third to updating and expanding the site.

Once your site is up and running, it's time to begin pulling in the visitors and prospects, and don't overlook your existing customers. You want them to use the site too.

You need a plan for your site's promotion and ongoing development, and you should consider a broad range of options:

- Marketing Promotion
  - Use traditional print promotion.
  - Use online promotion.
  - Broadcast your domain name.
  - Create search engine strategies.
  - Promote security.
- Advertising
  - Design banner ads.
  - Create alternatives to banners.
  - Calculate your allowable budget.
- Relationships
  - Develop reciprocal links.
  - Build co-marketing agreements.
  - Work with the competition.
  - Build global relationships.
- Ongoing Development
  - Apply creativity.
  - Create fresh content.
  - Expand your site.

MARKETING PROMOTION

If you build it, they won't come…unless you let people know who you are and where to find your Web site. All by itself, a Web site is passive. It sits there waiting to be found, waiting to educate, inform, entertain, and save your customers time and money. Only active marketing techniques will build interest and excitement. While you're promoting the sizzle, remember to stress the value of your site. Even a cool site needs a raison d'être today. Great graphics, video, and sound effects, as I've said before, do not constitute value. Tell your prospective customers how you can save them time and money. If your selection is the largest, broadcast that message.

Even if your marketing budget is the shoestring type, you cannot afford to ignore the many possible promotional avenues. If you apply a little creativity to the task, inexpensive marketing can be aggressive. In fact, this is the primary tenet of marketing. Here are 15 to get you started:

Every piece of paper that leaves your office must carry your Web address. Make your URL prominent on every brochure, piece of stationery, business card, and direct mail flyer. But don't stop there. Include your address on your statements, invoices, checks, notepads, and promotional giveaways. If you have T-shirts, canvas briefcases, coffee mugs, or pens emblazoned with your logo, add your Web address as well.

PUT YOUR EFFORT INTO EXISTING CUSTOMERS

While you need new customers to keep your business growing, don't take your loyal customers for granted. Providing exceptional customer service certainly is an important way to keep your customers happy, but they will also respond to your marketing efforts.

If you are wondering how best to allocate your limited time and money to marketing, try this formula: Devote 15 percent of your budget to attracting new, untried prospects. Your goal is to turn this audience into hot prospects. Allocate another 25 percent of your effort to converting hot prospects into buying customers. Finally, put the remaining 60 percent to work on those who have bought from you in the past. Assuming their previous experiences were good, past customers are the people most likely to buy from you again.

Your domain name is important. Select it carefully and make it virtually synonymous with the name of your business. For example, Amazon.com is both the company name and the Web address. Egghead Software believes this connection is so important it changed the name of the company to Egghead.com.

Select a Web address that is easy to remember and instantly associated with your business. This is equally important whether you are a start-up that needs to establish an image or a third-generation business owner with years invested in your brand.

If your business is called Ed's Auto Parts, and you are fortunate, you may be the first to apply for the URL www.edsautoparts.com. It's certainly easy for your customers to remember and, in this case, probably manageable (i.e., not too long to type accurately). If your name is already taken, you'll need an alternative. Select your alternate name carefully. For example, if you are not known well by your initials, avoid www.eap.com. Only companies like IBM, AT&T, or BMW, with recognizable initials, should try this. A better choice might be www.carparts.com or www.autosupply.com. While your name may not be part of the address, the connection to your business is obvious and might be a natural address for even a new prospect to try. You might try to secure www.edsautoparts.net as a final alternative. Although the .com suffix is every business's first choice, commercial sites can use .net. Even if you decide to promote yourself under a short, catchy domain name, such as www.ecar.com, secure your entire given name and link it to your site. A few people will always try to find you by name.

If your restaurant is called Uncle Luigi's Fine Italian Delicatessen, the odds are that no one will have your URL, but it may be a mistake for you to make this your primary domain name. You may want to secure the domain name, in case someone looks for you by typing in www.uncleluigisfineitaliandelicatessen.com, but such a long address increases the probability of error. You would be better served to choose a name that is short and to the point. You might try www.uncleluigi.com, www.thedeli.com, www.italiandeli.com, or www.pizzaatogo.com. Your domain name is important; give it as much thought as you did the name of your business.

Market to your employees. Your marketing department, management, and happy customers are not the only voices you have in the marketplace. Every member of your staff—to the last intern or summer employee—can bring in a sale, and there are several ways to engage your employees in marketing: First, keep morale high; happy employees improve your image and happy employees go the extra mile to serve your customers and prospects. Second, keep employees informed. When anyone on your staff is asked a question or is in a position to speak up on behalf of your company or products, you want that message to be accurate, as well as enthusiastic.

Give your employees samples of your merchandise to use at home. It's a terrific endorsement when a sales or customer service representative can say, "Well, my own experience suggests that you should..." or, "I use my widget every time I need to...." If you use an outside advertising agency or contract with a freelance writer or programmer, include these people in your internal marketing program. The cost is negligible in comparison to the potential returns.

Free *is as compelling on the Internet as it is in traditional business.* Whether you call it a loss leader, free consulting, a discount to members, free lifetime service, or a two-for-the-price-of-one special, give your customers something extra for buying from you. Entertainment alone is not enough to make people buy.

If you don't currently have a free service, create one. Try to create a service you only have to pay for once; then, a successful campaign won't bankrupt your business. For example, create an interactive utility or tool that customers can use free of charge anytime they want, as often as they want. Federal Express, probably more than any company, is responsible for bringing free service to the Internet. By developing its online tracking service, it has given customers the power to monitor delivery of a letter or package without calling a customer service representative.

Describe your online business in four or five sentences. Because these may be the most important sentences you ever write, take your time. Write and rewrite until you get it right. Start by making a list of all the key words that describe your business. For example, if you are an online travel agency, your key words might include *international, resorts, lowest airline fares, travel discounts, business trips*, and *charters*. Use these words when describing your business, and include them again as key words when you register with an online search engine. You might also want to include the names of your key competitors among your key search words. Then, when someone searches for ACME Travel, your business will come up in the search.

On the other hand, avoid empty adjectives. Words like *best, greatest,* and *oldest* will not help you. Even if you are the largest independent travel agency, a fact that is important to include on your site, it will not help your site to be found in an online search or adequately describe what you do.

List your site with the biggest and most popular search engines and directories. There are only 10 or 15 search engines you need to consider. It's fair to say that 90 percent of Web users rely on one of the top search engines, including Yahoo!, InfoSeek, AltaVista, Lycos, WebCrawler, Excite, Hot-Bot, and Ask Jeeves. If you prefer, you can contact each search tool separately, but you will probably find it easier (and a better use of your time) to register with a service like SubmitIt! (www.submit-it.com) or BizWiz! (www.bizwiz.com). You'll only need to fill out the forms once, and the service will submit the information to the leading search engines and directories for a small fee. You can update the information as often as you wish.

While services can make registering easier, be careful which service you select. Don't fall for promotions offering free submissions or services that promise to set you up on hundreds of search engines. In both cases, they may deliver what they promise, but you may not get the quality you expect. The submissions may be superficial, and the hundreds of search engines they choose will probably serve you no better than a carefully crafted listing on the top 20 or so services.

In addition to registering with the leading search engines, search the Web for specialty directories designed to promote your industry, your product line, or companies based in your geographic region.

After you have written your statement and registered your site with the leading search engines, test your effort. You may want to fine-tune your description and include some additional key words. Even if you get the results you want, you'll still need to continue testing every month or two. Your competition may have found new key words, and failure to add them to your site could cause your business to drop farther down in the list of search results. Update your description frequently.

Publish an e-letter. Even after visitors have found you, you still need to remind them to come back regularly. After all, more businesses are vying for your customers' online attention every day. Each month or quarter, send out an electronic newsletter (e-letter) that includes advice, suggestions, new products and services, special offers and discounts, and anything else that will interest your customers. Be sure to include links that transport the reader directly to related information on your Web site. Don't just link to your home page; link to a specific item. As you write your e-letter, keep your customers' interests in mind. Will they really want to know you just hired a new customer service manager or promoted Jane Smith to assistant vice president of marketing? Probably not. On the other hand, if you have just doubled the size of your customer service department to insure speedy response to requests and technical questions, this is news.

Keeping your messages brief will increase the likelihood that recipients will read your e-letter. If it's too long, reading it becomes work. Most people postpone reading long messages, or delete them unread.

Offering to send your free e-letter to everyone who signs up on your site also helps you build your mailing list while giving you legitimate access to more information about your customers and prospects. By asking the right questions at registration, you'll be better equipped to focus your content on customers' wants and immediate needs. If you can use this information to tailor your e-mail and e-letters to their specific requirements, you are providing people with an even greater service.

If you want to get a higher response to your e-letters, experiment with graphic-rich messages. They are more expensive and time-consuming to develop, but rather than sending customers a reminder to visit your site, you are, in effect, bringing your Web site to the customer.

Finally, you'll probably have a better response if you send your e-letter only to people who have requested it. Following this practice will help you avoid being boycotted or "flamed" (receiving hundreds of worthless e-mail messages that serve no purpose except to fill up your online mailbox).

Negotiate reciprocal links with companies and Web sites most likely to be popular with your target audience. If you sell rock-climbing equipment, look for climbing magazines and national parks online. Many rock climbers probably also enjoy other outdoor activities, such as white-water rafting and hang gliding, or they may be hikers and naturalists. They are also young, or at least think young.

If you target other business owners, look for trade associations, industry organizations, and corporate or small business sites your target prospects may visit. Perhaps there is a virtual trade show online, an educational institution, or a government or nonprofit organization that includes links to business sites serving its audience. Propose to the owners of these sites that you set up reciprocal links, but be careful how you display them. Don't hide the links, but don't make them the most prominent items on your Web site either. You don't want to risk losing new customers before you have a chance to introduce them to your site and what you are selling. Discuss with each prospective business or organization the potential for loading their sites into your Web site. Your Web developer can design your site to allow another site to come up inside a frame within your pages or in a separate window. In either case, visitors won't actually leave your site to view the others.

How will you know which links you should pursue? Conduct a few searches with your own key words (using several different search engines), then make a list of the sites that come up consistently among the top 20 or so. These are all sites you should consider linking with.

Test online classified advertising. In an effort to win higher visitation numbers, some sites offer visitors the opportunity to post their classified

ads free of charge. Others may have a small fee attached. Look for classified ad sites that receive heavy visitation, come up at the top of the list in
online searches, and are promoted through banner ads. Then post your ad to
sell something directly or to point prospective customers to your Web site.
It's not a sure-fire winner, but it certainly cannot hurt.

***Join Internet news groups, chat rooms, and mailing lists that your
prospects visit.*** Most experts recommend this tactic. If you can promote
your site to people who will find your business interesting, it's a good
avenue to pursue. But there are a couple of downsides you need to consider.
First, this is a time-consuming tactic. You have to spend time on these sites,
entering into the online discussions, demonstrating your expertise, and
sharing your knowledge. Second, what you write must have value. You
can't simply join in and start with blatant promotions of your business. By
their very nature, news groups and mailing lists are not commercial. They
are places where people come together to share ideas and network. Participants are looking for real value, not advertisements.

One solution may be to include online participation in the job description of one of your more Web-savvy employees. Make it her job to communicate regularly with other news group and chat room members. Encourage
him to share his knowledge freely. If messages can be posted, have your
employees create an e-mail template that includes a sentence or two at the
bottom that lists the name of your business, an e-mail contact, telephone
number, and your URL. Think of this as a mini-advertisement that follows
constructive advice. Be aware that the advertisement used alone will get you
in trouble with most news group members. If they think you are just promoting yourself at their expense, they'll get even. They may "flame" your
site with hundreds of worthless e-mail messages or encourage other members to boycott your company's Web site. You'll end up creating more ene-
mies and pushing your prospects into the waiting arms of your competition.

Remember, a news group is not a free mailing list. You should not start
broadcasting (or "spamming") your promotions to the other participants.
Let them come to you.

Post your Web address on all your display advertising. Whether in print, television, or radio, if you are a Web-based business, this is essential. If you use your Web site as an extension of your offline business, you should treat your URL with the same importance and attention as you do your 800 number and address.

Join an online shopping mall or trade directory. By participating in the right mall—one with good marketing and operational programs—you can benefit from a certain economy of scale. The advantage is that all members' fees are working together to collectively promote your location. Among the better malls, the site owners promote their sites aggressively, which will help bring people to you. If the mall limits participation to selected industries (such as travel, business-to-business, apparel, etc.), people will come to the mall expecting the products and services you offer. Because malls are virtual shopping centers, your service provider will still host your site (or it will remain on your own server).

Some Internet Service Providers also provide their own free directories and mall listings. This is another way they can build a critical mass of visitors, which they in turn can sell to advertisers.

A more recent trend among some larger companies is to offer free participation in their mall or directory. For example, your bank or insurance company may offer to post your site (or at the very least give you a directory listing with a hot link). These links are usually free to customers, so take advantage of them.

Buy a targeted e-mail list. While I am not an advocate of unsolicited, untargeted e-mail, I do believe that direct mail (whether online or print) can be effective. As online marketing becomes more sophisticated, you'll find it increasingly easy to purchase lists of prospects who 1) have agreed to receive targeted e-mail and 2) have been profiled to match your target audience. These recipients will be predisposed to receiving your promotional message and, therefore, more likely to act.

Don't promote beyond your capacity to fulfill. If you have read much about
the spike in online shopping during the 1999 holiday season, you may have
noticed the mixed accounts regarding customer satisfaction. Most online
shoppers were delighted to be able to use the Internet as an alternative to
fighting the Christmas throng at the local mall. However, you can also read
about downtime of various popular Web sites and overloads that slowed
transaction processing to a crawl. A few businesses received more orders
than they had product to sell. Orders backed up, and some friends and family members received promises rather than presents under the tree.

The lesson is simple: If you want to move slowly online and not invest
all your capital in inventory and order processing personnel, don't overpro-
mote your site. Determining the right amount of promotion is a very individual task. No two sites have exactly the same issues and potential
problems. Just move forward cautiously, and remember that you can have
too much of a good thing. If your order processing and customer service
fail to satisfy, customers will be reluctant to give you a second chance.
Unfortunately, this is not an exact science; you'll have to use your offline
experience, common sense, and testing to judge the right amount of promotion for your business.

Never stop promoting your site. Experts estimate that the number of number of Web sites doubles every 100 days. You can't run the risk of losing out
to newer sites that are marketing more aggressively. You need to keep your
promotional efforts as fresh and powerful as your content.

Integrate your Web promotion into your traditional business marketing. If
you follow this rule, you'll never overlook your Web site or treat it like a poor
relation. In addition to online promotional efforts, rely on the tried and true.
For example, issue press releases announcing your online presence. Be sure
to send copies to the editors of all the Internet magazines as well as the online
Web news services. You could receive some free publicity in a listing of
"cool" Web sites or new sites. If an editor or freelance writer does a story of
Web sites in your industry, you might find your site displayed prominently.

THE FEDEX APPROACH

Federal Express Corporation (FedEx) opened many entrepreneurs' eyes to the potential of the World Wide Web when the company brought its tracking utilities to the Internet in November 1994. In the process of opening e-commerce and e-business to more clients, FedEx helped pave the way for many other businesses to find commercial success on the Web and solve customers' demand for instant gratification. Careful observation demonstrates that marketing has played an important and carefully managed role in FedEx's online strategy, and that many of its tactics have been innovative.

FedEx came to the Internet with a wealth of experience and a very substantial part of its business already facilitated through its FedEx Power-Ship® program. Introduced over a decade ago, FedEx PowerShip® literally gave customers the hardware and proprietary software they needed to automate shipment preparation and track shipments. In 1994, when the Internet was gaining momentum and problems of reliability and security were being solved, FedEx moved onto the Internet as a platform. It set up a Web page linked to its automated tracking capability. In the years since, the lines between FedEx's proprietary network and the Internet have blurred so that the difference is transparent to customers.

FedEx had never promoted its tracking service heavily, but within a year on the Internet, tracking requests multiplied. One of the advantages of having a strong brand was that, as people become more Internet savvy, "fedex.com" was a natural address to go to. When its competitors promoted their technology capabilities, FedEx benefited from the halo effect.

Since first offering its tracking capability online, the company has added significantly to its capabilities. It seems likely that the electronic interface will eventually be the primary and preferred way to do business with FedEx, and that everything other than the physical pick-up and delivery of the shipment will be accomplished online.

Although tracking is one of the most important capabilities, the main customer interface with FedEx is in shipping preparation. FedEx speeded up this process through its proprietary network, then added the capability of preprinting airbills to its Internet site with a feature called FedEx inter-NetShip, beginning with domestic only coverage and later expanding to global shipping. Customers can now dispatch a courier directly from the FedEx site, or they can look up the closest drop-off location and drop packages off themselves.

At first FedEx did very little to promote FedEx interNetShip beyond including references to its home page in normal marketing materials. The quality of its service—and the enviable perception that FedEx is the way to send a critically important package—seems to have been the company's most effective form of marketing.

Making customers part of the development process is also good marketing. From its Internet beginnings, FedEx used customer feedback and online questionnaires to understand how its customers used the Web site and what their experiences were. Those who provided feedback were invited to be alpha testers and beta testers for FedEx interNetShip.

What customers like about FedEx is this: If you are tracking a package, no matter where in the world it is going, FedEx supports the shipment. As FedEx interNetShip expanded globally, the company worked to develop sites that were relevant to customers in each country, to give their global customers an experience appropriate to the local experience. FedEx has rolled out local content and native language support country by country, and its more than 145,000 employees around the world take an active role in creating a medium with global reach and local relevance.

FedEx has focused on the commerce, rather than the electronic, in "electronic commerce." As a result, many customers are coming to them for help with all of their electronic commerce needs.

The real marketing advantage in e-commerce is its potential for personalization. Facilitating companies' capability to deliver custom orders is a real boon to start-ups that want to compete with larger, more established companies. It helps companies use the Internet as a wonderful marketing tool. The leading online companies are moving beyond mass marketing to one-to-one marketing. A company can build a profile of each customer and use that information to create an experience that's relevant to each and every customer. When this is paired with flexible manufacturing, the power is incredible. These companies are saying, "You can have it your way; we will fulfill it your way."

The lesson to be learned from the FedEx experience is that using the Web is not a technology problem but a marketing problem: How do you use the Internet to create value for your customers so that they want to do business with you? The technology is only a facilitator. In traditional business, marketers used direct mail with bounce-back cards or, more intrusively, telemarketing. For more in-depth contact, a customer might be selected to participate in a focus group or telephone interview. By contrast, the Internet enables business owners to have a dialogue with customers every day, if they want to, and in real time.

OTHER GOOD EXAMPLES

Here are some sites to view to start identifying marketing tools:

- Innovative Internet Marketing Solutions: http://www.iimsnet. com/home.htm

- Advanced Internet Marketing: http://www.aim2.com/

- Netwatchers Cyberzine: http://www.emitech.com/ netwatchers/front.htm

- AdNews: http://www.adnews.com/

- Guerrilla Marketing Online: http://www.gmarketing.com/

- Cyberwave Media: http://www.cyberwave.com/index.html

- Web Marketing Today: http://www.wilsonweb.com/ rfwilson/articles/attract.htm

SEARCH ENGINE STRATEGIES: FIND AND BE FOUND

Every time I talk about the Internet, questions invariably arise about searching for information, conducting research online, and improving the chances of others finding your Web site. The Internet is the source of a wealth of information on an almost infinite number of subjects, with content produced by people around the world. The challenge for every Web user is finding useful information. The Internet is not a library with every document and every Web site identified systematically and logically. There is no Dewey Decimal System for the Internet. With new sites coming online at a rate of thousands per day and the Web doubling in size every 100 days, it is important for business owners to make search engine strategies part of their marketing plans.

You must use search engines effectively to support your need for industry and competitive research and establish your site with the major search engines as effectively as possible (with the goal of being found when customers and prospects come looking). An understanding of search engines and directories is important to any discussion of online marketing.

Search engines use software programs (called spiders, crawlers, robots, and worms) to find and compile lists of domain names. The index (the meat of the database) is built from titles, full text, size, URL, links, and so forth. The selection criteria are then used to query the index and return the best matches possible.

- *AltaVista* (www.altavista.com) is a large database of Web sites and Usenet newsgroups that can be searched using advanced Boolean logic.

- *Deja News* (www.dejanews.com) is known as the Discussion Network. Users can read, search, participate in, and subscribe to more than 80,000 discussion forums and Usenet newsgroups.

- *Excite* (www.excite.com) is a large database that supports concept searching to help users narrow the range of a search.

- *GoTo* (www.goto.com) has been built around the original World Wide Web Worm and incorporates newer technology that supports competitive bidding and user evaluations.

- *HotBot* (www.hotbot.com) searches are made easy with the help of form-based Boolean tools.

- *Inference Find* (www.inference.com) goes beyond the typical search to actively try to provide conversation-based, knowledge-driven answers and solutions.

- *InfoSeek* (www.infoseek.com) is among the more popular search engines. It includes Web sites, Usenet newsgroups, Reuters news, and company profiles.

- *The Internet Sleuth* (www.isleuth.com) is a powerful search engine that also supports an iSleuth Shopper section and awards digital currency as loyalty points.

- *Lycos* (www.lycos.com) supports Boolean and proximity searches.

- *MetaCrawler* (www.go2net.com/search) is embedded in the Go2Net site to support powerful meta-site searches.

- *MetaFind* (www.metafind.com) supports a variety of options for listing matches according to date, alphabetical order, and more.

- *Northern Light* (www.northernlight.com) includes access to more than free information. It includes access to a Special Collection of fee-based articles.

- *PlanetSearch* (www.planetsearch.com) is something of a hybrid between a directory and a search engine. It includes listings of yellow pages, white pages, government data, and topics of special interest.

- *ProFusion* (www.profusion.com) is supported by the University of Kansas and provides point-and-click options to search and rank by number of links and whether or not to include summaries. Users can select several other search engines to be called into the search.

- *Reference.com* (www.reference.com) includes Usenet newsgroups, mailing lists, and Web forums that can be searched using advanced Boolean logic.

- *Web Crawler* (www.webcrawler.com) is one of the oldest search engines.

Search engines and directories can help you navigate the length and breadth of the Internet. They help customers narrow a search and even rank the matches according to their relevance. Alas, they are far from perfect tools. For example, their ability to ask for more information is limited. These tools rely on the person conducting the search to be as specific as possible, and on the Web site owners to carefully select and enter the key words and other descriptors that will help them be found.

The two keys to being found are *location* and *frequency*. In other words, where you position your key words and how often you use them rule a search engine's judgment in creating a match and ranking it. Anyone who has conducted an online search knows that search engines can return tens of thousands of matches, out of which we typically look no farther than the first 20 or so listings.

Understand what each search engine is looking for. Some of the requirements are universal; others are unique to a particular engine. All search engines rely on location. Just as you would go to the library and search first by title, so too do search engines. Pages with key words appearing in the title are considered most on-target. Next, search engines scan any headlines or initial passages looking for a match. Again, the closer to the beginning the key words fall, the more relevant they are assumed to be.

While location will get your Web site included in a search, frequency helps determine its ranking. Most search engines count the number of times a key word appears. The higher the frequency, the more relevant the site. At the same time, Web designers are always looking for ways to trick a search engine into giving their sites an advantage. In your effort to compete, be careful that you do not turn frequency in search engine spamming. In this case, spamming refers to repeating a key word dozens, even hundreds, of times in a row. Most search engines are aware of this tactic and may actually penalize sites caught using this technique.

FIGURE 8-1 This chart lists the features of some of the most popular search engines and directories.

Search Engine or Directory	URL	Usefulness	Limitations	Case Sensitive	Boolean Logic	Fields	Phrases	Truncation Support
Infoseek	www.infoseek.com	Accurate and quick processing with frequent updates to the database and clustering of results.	Tends to return many irrelevant hits along with the right ones; the database is smaller than that of many search engines.	Full case sensitivity	*Or* is default; implied logic: + for *and*, – for *not*.	Title, URL, Site, and Link	Supported in double quote marks or with hyphens between each word.	No symbol; stems each term.
AltaVista	www.altavista.digi-tal.com	Features a very large database, allows for complex searches, and supports searches in many languages.	Boolean logic will switch in a search of multiple fields; weak relevancy assessment.	Full case sensitivity	*Or* is default; implied logic: + for *and*, – for *not*.	Anchor, Applet, Domain, Host, Image, Link, Text, Title, URL	Supported in double quote marks.	Required; uses*; supports internal truncation.
HotBot	www.hotbot.com	Very large database and support for complex Boolean searches and special fields.	Truncation is not supported and relevancy ranking is weak.	Limited support within words	Logic supported with terms in template; supports logic in phrases.	Page title, continent, date, media types	Supported in double quote marks.	None
Excite	www.excite.com	Searches by concept, key word, and natural language as well as Boolean logic.	Concept hits may have limited relevancy; no field searches are available.	None	*Or* is default; implied logic: + for *and*, – for *not*.	None	Supported in double quote marks.	None

Search Engine or Directory	URL	Usefulness	Limitations	Case Sensitive	Boolean Logic	Fields	Phrases	Truncation Support
Lycos	www.lycos.com	The very current database supports a variety of Boolean terms and proximity options.	Its database is smaller than many and not a full text-based search.	None	*And* is default; implied logic: + for *and*, – for *not*.	Title, URL, Site	Supported in double quote marks.	Optional symbol $; stems search terms; period prevents truncation.
The Argus Clearinghouse	www.clearing-house.net	Sites and information have been reviewed by subject experts. Tends to focus on academic subjects.	Searching syntax tends to be a little quirky.	None	Full Boolean logic; no support for *not*; *and* is default.	None	None	Required; uses*
Yahoo!	www.yahoo.com	Require a broad-based view of a topic—breadth and depth. Good for commercial coverage	No evaluation and far from comprehensive. Does not typically index secondary pages. Each advanced search supports only a single Boolean operator.	None	*And* is default.	Title and URL	Supported in double quote marks.	Required; uses*
Magellan	www.mckinley.com	Greater effort to be comprehensive, and better coverage of academic topics. Includes reviews.	Not always up to date on a topic.	None	Full Boolean logic; *or* is default.	None	Supported in double quote marks.	None

No two searches for the same words on different search engines will return the same results. For one thing, if a Web site owner has not registered his or her site with a search engine, it won't be found. Second, each search engine has its own rules and idiosyncrasies. As an example of a rule is how the engine uses Boolean logic (the use of *and, not,* and other words used to qualify a search). An example of an idiosyncrasy is the way an engine uses links to determine popularity. When a site has many other sites pointing, or linking, to it, the site is deemed a better match than one with fewer pointers.

Some search engines are actually hybrids that include both the features of a directory and those of a search engine. Content is originally selected because it matches the general parameters of the subjects included in the directory. Some directories actually review sites and their content, and those receiving a higher rating earn a higher match ranking when the directory is searched. It's an imperfect system, but the intention is to give Web users the best possible assistance.

Many Web designers believe that embedding key words in a site's meta tags (including blocks of key words in the HTML programming language but hiding them from view) will boost the site to the top of a search. This is not the secret weapon in the battle to be found. InfoSeek does favor meta tags; Excite, on the other hand, does not read them at all. A site completely lacking in meta tags can receive a high rank in a match.

DIRECTORIES

As important as search engines are in the quest for answers online, directories (and increasingly hybrid directories that support full Boolean searches) can be a Web user's best friend. Because directories are organized by subject, you must first find the right directory. You also must understand that a directory is only as good as the information it includes. Typically, the staff of universities, libraries, companies, associations, and organizations are responsible for the selections. Many pass value judgments on the worthiness of a site to be included in their directory.

Like search engines, directories differ significantly in content. No two directories contain the exact same data. Their policies for inclusion and review also vary, although most accept (or at least consider) submissions. As with search engines, submissions need to be updated and resubmitted regularly. The rules for determining rank in a search, however, differ not only from search engines but among directories. Study the requirements of each directory you decide to target.

While far from comprehensive, this list describes several of the better-known directories available online. These directories typically support a broad range of topics:

- *The Argus Clearinghouse* (www.clearinghouse.net) is considered one of the top directories and a valuable tool for academics. Specialists in each topic review and rate content before it is listed.

- *BUBL Link* (bubl.ac.uk/link) is an academic directory supported by the University of Strathclyde Library in Glasgow, Scotland. Data is classified using the Dewey Decimal classification system.

- *eBLAST* (www.britannica.com) is managed by the editors of *Encyclopedia Britannica,* who classify, rate, and review all sites. Their intent is to provide links to what they consider the best sites on the World Wide Web.

- *Galaxy* (galaxy.einet.net) contains a broad range of topics of use to business professionals. Although America's Health Network sponsors the site, content is not limited to health-related topics.

- *Infomine* (infomine.ucr.edu) is another scholarly directory, this one compiled at the University of California at Riverside. Content includes electronic books, journals, bulletin boards, listservs, library card catalogs, databases, and articles aimed at the needs of students and faculty.

- *InfoSurf* (www.library.ucsb.edu/index.html) is focused on the needs of University of California, Santa Barbara faculty and students. In addition to being an extension of the university library, it contains content related to the campus community at large.

- *Lycos Top 5%* (point.lycos.com/categories) is the result of further examination of sites included in the Lycos search engine. Commercial, public, and private sites are all eligible; the only criteria is quality of content.

- *PINAKES, A Subject Launchpad* (www.hw.ac.uk/libwww/irn/pinakes/pinakes.html) is a small directory with lofty goals. It takes its name from the catalog system developed by Callimachus for the ancient University of Alexandria. The directory is a collection of meta-sites organized by subject.

- *Scout Report Signpost* (www.signpost.org/signpost) supports a broad range of topics that can be browsed or searched using Library of Congress classifications.

- *The WWW Virtual Library* (vlib.stanford.edu/overview.html) numbers among the original online directories. Much of its content comes from universities worldwide.

- *Yahoo!* (www.yahoo.com) is without question the best known and most widely used directory on the Web. Although sites are accepted without review, the breadth of the content and powerful search capabilities have helped to propel this service to the top.

THE POWER OF INFORMATION

You've already heard from James E. Coane, President and COO of CDnow. He has firsthand insight into the promotional value of helping customers get real answers. This is not a conventional approach to marketing, but rather good common sense. He discusses the good news and bad news of the vast data available online and stresses the need for companies to provide tools that enable customers to get answers to their buying questions as easily and effortlessly as possible.

> *Almost anything you can find in a university or major public library is available on the Internet today. Everything from the most risqué adult stuff to the most esoteric scientific research is out there. The biggest problem is finding the information or company you want. It can be a slow,*

painful process, particularly for people relatively new to the Internet.

The media have so overhyped the Internet that new users who have never had any exposure come to it with very high expectations. They are more likely to be disappointed than wowed. They actually find the size and breadth of the Internet intimidating. Watch television commercials these days and you would think this stuff has been around for the last ten years, and all you have to do is connect. Not so. As someone who has grown up in the technology, I am pleasantly surprised every day by how rapidly the developments are occurring. But the uninitiated can be frustrated by the whole idea of working with a computer and a mouse.

How will your prospects navigate this environment? The good news is the trend toward organizing information topically, much the way you would find information organized in a library.

Search engines "crawl" the Web, identifying and indexing sites that people can search using simple key words and concepts. This capability enables both business and lifestyle decisions. With a little effort, Web users can find everything from information about planning a vacation or business trip to booking a hotel reservation to researching restaurants to researching the many conferences and association events available.

The good news is that you have access to all this information. The bad news is that you could spend the rest of your life finding it. And the process of finding what you're looking for creates many opportunities to be distracted. Not only will people spend more time online than they planned, but you may lose a sale because a prospect gets sidetracked. Effective use of search tools will help, but some of the more innovative delivery technologies go beyond the search tool. For example, Web users can set up their own information profiles and have pertinent information delivered in real time. My Yahoo, My Excite, and CBS Marketwatch are such services. At the same time, more credible, reliable content is on the Web and at very affordable prices—from free to very affordable. These sources include the New York Times, Washington Post and the Wall Street Journal and other newspapers from the major chains—Gannett, USA Today, Times Mirror, and Knight-Ridder.

So you have this huge, evolving resource that is rich in terms of content and acceptability. But the decision maker's mantra remains: I want it fast, I want it cheap, I want it now, and I want my answer, not data. In addition to serving as a new content environment, the Internet is a new communications environment, and it enables companies to link their internal information with external information to create an interactive resource to support decision making, which is very new. The closest thing previously was groupware and workflow software, such as Lotus Notes. But these required a greater investment in money and equipment than many small businesses could afford.

We promote, market, and sell music and related merchandise, but in order to do so we make it easier for customers to decide what to buy. We do this by packaging highly reliable, highly recognized, dependable content into information utilities and applications that are targeted to meet the very specific needs of our customers.

Every business' customers want the ability to scan across multiple sources of information and get the results packaged for them in a form that is as close to an answer as one can get without having to do all that work. That's what we provide. Content is rapidly evolving from the presentation of textual information, to graphics and sound samples that can be searched, to something that looks more like TV programming. For the Web entrepreneur, the ability to link back into transaction-supported services and shopping makes the business opportunities exciting.

There's no magic bullet. If anything, it's even more difficult to succeed online, because differentiation becomes critical when customers are just a click away from the competition. There are many issues to confront in this new world. We are betting that it's going to be worth it.

Tips for Finding Information Online

- *Select a search engine that supports the types of search options that will best serve your needs.* If you decide to use a directory, identify one that includes your primary category. For example, if you want commercial information, start with a directory like Lycos Top 5% or Yahoo!.

- *Remember that no search engine is comprehensive.* They are updated regularly, but don't expect up-to-the-minute data to be included. Also, most search engines cannot index files inside password-protected sites or located behind a company's firewall. If a site is not linked to other sites, many search engines overlook it.

- *If you are new to a search engine, read the directions.* You can certainly use a search engine without reading the directions, but if you want to fashion your search to deliver the best possible matches, it pays to read the directions. Also, look into the advanced search strategies that most sites support. Remember that what works on one directory or search engine may not work on another.

- *Identify basic concepts for your search.* For example, if you want to search NASA's efforts to explore the planets in our galaxy, your concepts will include planets, NASA, and space exploration.

- *Make a list of key words that fall under each concept or might further refine your ability to find precise information.* For planets, key words would include Neptune, Mars, Jupiter, Saturn, and so on. Under space exploration, you might want to identify space flights by name or use a more generic term like unmanned missions. The concept NASA opens up key word options including the names of NASA directors, budget, policies, and so on.

- *Check support for case-sensitive searches.* Some search engines support capitalization of words. If this is the case, using "Booth Tarkington" rather than "booth tarkington" will help limit results to those about the author Booth Tarkington and eliminate useless links to toll booths and many other types of booths.

- *Apply Boolean logic to define relationships among key words.* The terms or logical operators *and*, *or*, and *not* help refine a search and improve the ranking results of matches. Here are three examples of the terms at work:

FIGURE 8-2

Search Statement	Results
cars *and* trains	All documents in the database that include both the words cars and trains
cars *or* trains	All documents in the database that include either cars *or* trains (both do not need to be present)
cars *not* trains	All documents in the database that include cars and, at the same time, do not include trains

Note that some search engines use an implied form of Boolean logic that employs symbols or spaces to indicate the operations (such as +dogs +cats to implement *dogs **and** cats*). In the case of the phrase *infant toys*, if it is not limited by quotation marks, some search engines could interpret it as *infant **and** toys*.

- *Apply a proximity operator.* A proximity operator is a refinement of the *and* operator. The term *near* requires that the key words be closely tied, typically not separated by more than five to ten words. Several search engines even allow the user to define the maximum distance between words. *Near* is very useful when you want to narrow results. Rather than a list of all matches with your key words, you will receive only those in which the terms appear close to one another. For example, "saturn *near* budget" will most likely give you results about the cost and budget allocations of the Saturn missions.

- *Search by field to help limit results.* In search engines that support full-text files, you can narrow your results by specifying where you expect the key word to appear. For example, *Title:*elephant will only return matches with the word elephant in the title. Equally handy is the ability to search terms in the URL field.

- *Be prepared to test different combinations to achieve maximum results.* Most search engines do not support every option. Therefore you will need to test different combinations of concepts and key words and logical operators. You can expect to get different results from each effort.

- *If you receive too few results, try to broaden the search.* Drop concept words. Connect terms with *or* instead of *and*. Test alternative spellings. Try a different search engine, preferably one that will search more than one directory simultaneously.

- *Test the results you receive from both the simple and advanced search options.* Each operates differently and supports different options. You may also find that one type or the other better suits the way you think.

Tips for Web Site Developers

In addition to understanding the search strategies your prospective visitors will use, you can apply some simple steps to improve your chances of being found. Here are a few ideas:

- *Write a page title.* Write a descriptive title of five to eight words for each page. Remove filler words from the title, such as *the*, or *and*. This page title appears on the Web search engines when your page is found. Entice surfers to click on the title by making it a bit provocative. Place it at the top of the Web page, between the `<HEADER></HEADER>` tags, in this format: `<TITLE>Web Marketing Checklist—23 Ways to Promote Your Site</TITLE>`

- *List keywords.* Prepare a list of 50 to 100 keywords. Think of all the words that you'd like your site to be found by. Make sure that you don't repeat any word more than three times. Place those words at the top of the Web page, between the `<HEADER></HEADER>` tags, in a meta tag in this format: `<META NAME="KEYWORDS" CONTENT="promoting, promotion, Web marketing, online sales ...">`

- *Write a page description.* Select the twenty most important key words and write a careful, 200- to 250-character (including spaces) sentence or two. Don't repeat any words used in the page title. Keep the description readable but tight. Eliminate as many filler words as you can, to make room for the key words, which do the actual work for you. Place those words at the top of the Web page, between the `<HEADER>` `</HEADER>` tags, in a meta tag in this format: `<META NAME= "DESCRIPTION" CONTENT="Increase visitor hits, attracting traffic through submitting URLs, META tags, news releases, banner ads, and reciprocal links">`

- *Submit your page to search engines and directories with the help of a service.* A submission service such as Submit-It (www.submit-it.com) or All4one Submission Machine (www.all4one.com/all4submit) can make it easier to post your site with the most important search engines.

ONLINE SECURITY AS A MARKETING TOOL

One of the reasons Web users cited in 1996 for limiting their use of the Internet to surfing and viewing free information was that they were afraid online transactions might compromise their privacy and credit information. These issues have been addressed in both perception and reality, which is reflected in the fact that 20 million people do business online today.

The vast and unfamiliar territory of the Internet is frightening to those who do not fully understand how it works but recognize the potential for widespread abuse involving credit card information. The irony is that many of the same people freely recite their credit card information to strangers over the telephone, a practice that is far from secure.

Security management should be approached as a multilayer effort:

- *Step One* is to develop a solid understanding of the potential security pitfalls and threats. By design, the Internet is structured as a public forum, so there is no inherent security on the Web or in most other kinds of Net interaction.

- *Step Two* is the strategic application of technology. In addition to secure technology, use a strategy of firewalls and secure e-business to separate personal and financial information away from the open Internet, and encrypt all electronic orders prior to transmission. Through the ongoing development of secure payment mechanisms, multiparty protocols, firewalls, industry standards, and other new technologies, online transactions are becoming increasingly safe.

- *Step Three* is to include a policy statement and prominent references to your use of security measures on your Web site. That will do a lot to boost confidence in your site.

"When it comes to securing Internet transactions, the good news is that the technology does indeed exist," reports Robert O. Babcock, Industry Segment Executive, IBM Small and Medium Business. "In fact, much of it has been in place for years." The cornerstone of secured transactions, called the Digital Encryption Standard, was developed by IBM in the late 1970s and is still used to secure millions of ATM transactions every day.

IBM and other major developers of Internet e-commerce services, including MasterCard and Visa, have developed and adopted the Secure Electronic Transaction™ (SET) protocol. SET technology is built into the IBM Payment Suite of products, which includes the IBM Consumer Wallet and IBM Payment Server.

Consumers can use the Consumer Wallet to store electronic payment card information and review their accounts. The IBM Consumer Wallet, formerly known as IBM CommercePOINT Wallet, as a browser plug-in that provides everything needed to shop with confidence on the World Wide Web: enhanced security, SET protocol utilization, more convenience, and transaction routing (including certification).

The electronic wallet is an easy-to-use depiction of a wallet that provides safe storage of electronic payment cards and related information. The wallet makes it easy to manage electronic payment card activities. It also contains a personal "digital signature" that helps secure each transaction.

You can easily add or remove cards from the wallet. (This doesn't delete the transactions already made with card, however.) You can even edit card names to separate business and personal transactions made with the same card. You are notified if any of your cards have expired or if their credit terms have been revoked.

The IBM Consumer Wallet application can't be launched without first entering your personal password or PIN, so your payment cards get an extra level of protection to help keep them safe.

Companies wanting to offer secure credit card transaction processing can use IBM Payment Server, which even allows businesses to forward customer card data to the bank via SET.

Digital Alternatives

IBM is helping to expand the scope of Internet payments by participating in the development and implementation of an electronic check pilot program for the U.S. Treasury sponsored by the Financial Services Technology Consortium (FSTC). IBM Research has successfully built an Electronic Check Bank Server for the U.S. Treasury's 12-month market trial electronic check program, which allows commercial banks to receive, sort, and validate electronic checks. The Electronic Check Bank Server seamlessly integrates with a bank's legacy check processing and payment systems and sends electronic check information to banks for settlement. IBM intends to continue to enhance its Electronic Check Bank Server by adding significant features and functions, and has plans to integrate it into the IBM Payment Suite™ of Internet payment products.

The FSTC developed the electronic check project as part of its ongoing effort to introduce new technologies into the U.S. banking system that benefit financial institutions, businesses, and consumers. The inherent security features built into the system's design satisfy the U.S. Treasury's stringent requirements for security. The electronic check solution incorporates the familiar banking standards for check processing and payment while providing ease of entry into one of the fastest growing markets—electronic commerce. Because the electronic check builds on the existing paper check infrastructure, consumers, businesses, and government will be able to use their current checking accounts to extend to the Internet.

Several years ago, the FSTC began research and development on the electronic check initiative. IBM was there. On June 30, 1998 the U.S. Government made its first electronic payment over the Internet using an electronic check. IBM was there. By the year 2000, the FSTC expected to have a full-scale rollout of electronic checks. IBM will be there as a key participant in this new and exciting Internet payment solution. IBM is helping more businesses become e-businesses by extending their existing payment methods to the Internet.

DIGITAL ADVERTISING: IS IT WORTH IT?

With each advancement in secure transaction processing and each new user who comes online, the opportunities for doing business expand. "When I think of the Internet's potential," says IBM's Peter Rowley, "I envision millions of people researching every imaginable product and service and buying through secured transactions."

A growing number of banner ads are appearing on favorite online search tools (such as Yahoo!, Infoseek, and Lycos) and on popular Web sites promoting everything from Walt Disney to AT&T to IBM. Banner ads are the narrow bands, typically located at the top and bottom of a Web page, that serve small, eye-catching display ads and a hot link to the advertiser's site. Companies that develop high-traffic sites are vying to attract ad dollars in order to offset some of their development costs and create revenue.

Today, major worldwide advertisers are blazing the way in banner advertising. If we look at dollars spent on online advertising as reported by the Internet Advertising Bureau and Pricewaterhouse Coopers LLP, we see strong growth. During the second quarter of 1998, advertisers spent $423 million, which represents an increase of 97 percent over the same quarter 1997. It's also the ninth consecutive quarter of positive growth.

To date, however, small businesses have not been big users of Web advertising, accounting for just two percent of the $1 billion spent in 1999. One reason for their reticence, explains *BusinessWeek*, is that small business advertising needs are typically regional. This may change as more small businesses fully realize the Internet's capacity to help them target broader audiences. At the same time, online advertisers are beginning to

---

THE PRICE OF A BANNER AD IS FALLING

If you are considering either running a banner ad to attract business to your Web site or selling ad space on your site, AdKnowledge Inc. provides some numbers that will help you to price your offer or evaluate the rates you are being charged. You'll notice that the average cost to reach 1,000 people has declined slightly. Also, remember that the largest sites—those demonstrating the greatest traffic—have the best chance of winning the still somewhat limited dollars being directed into online advertising.

Date	Average Cost to Reach 1,000 Visitors
March 1997	$39.10
June 1997	$39.60
September 1997	$39.20
December 1997	$37.20
January 1998	$37.36
February 1998	$37.43
March 1998	$36.63
April 1998	$37.29
May 1998	$37.84

---

package and sell regional offerings. The rates are lower, reflecting the restricted distribution of the ads, and are well within the price range of smaller businesses. Whether your primary goal is to sell your own products and services or to build a readership that reflects your target market profile, opportunities to attract advertisers exist.

When developing a strategy to attract advertising, business owners should think of their sites as an infrastructure for distributing information. The higher the demand for the information, the more traffic the site will enjoy, making it attractive to advertisers. It's the same principle magazines and television networks use to sell advertising: The more popular a magazine or television show, the more viewers the producers can offer advertisers, who will pay top dollar to be seen.

With computer- and consumer-related advertising leading the way, financial services, new media, and telecommunications are close behind. "The continuing growth of online advertising revenue only reaffirms the vitality of the medium as an increasingly important component for advertisers' campaigns," said IAB Chairman Rich LeFurgy. "We are seeing increasing numbers of large advertisers integrate online spending into their overall media plans, which is a significant boost for the medium. Additionally, the industry is experiencing a surge of interest from all quarters—agencies, advertisers, publishers, technology enablers, and research companies—geared toward improving the performance of online advertising for the mutual benefit of all."

For all the reported growth, banner advertising has its detractors in the industry, no doubt frightening many potential advertisers away. What's the answer? Where is the best place to spend your advertising budget? The answer depends on several issues, and much of the negative reporting is a carryover from an earlier market. The fact is, just a couple of years ago (before the Web became entrenched in our minds and the numbers of online users began to reach a critical mass), many people took offense to the commercialization of the Web. Their response to banner advertising was negative.

But the online market has changed. People online today take advertising for granted. Now the challenge is, in part, to find the best sites to place one's ads (sites with large numbers of viewers who match a business' target market). In addition, companies must develop creative ads that capture the attention and interest of viewers and make them want to click through. The time has come for the same degree of creativity to be applied to banner advertising as is applied to print, television, and radio ads. There's one more thing to consider: The Web is so pervasive today that all forms of advertising must make reference to a company's Web site. While it once made sense to focus on advertising to the people already online, today the inclusion of Web promotion in traditional media will actually help to draw more people to the Web. Each business owner must assess the power of his or her Web-based advertising.

BANNERS GET A BAD RAP

"Banners get a bad rap," admits Yahoo!'s Tim Koogle, "but from what we've seen they are effective. As the ad agencies become more comfortable with this medium, their efforts become more dynamic and powerful. Just as they've learned how to place creative ads, they've learned where to place their banner ads to get maximum attention.

"Like all other media, advertising has to pop, and it has to be placed where it will be seen by someone who will consider it relevant.

"In addition to the banner, a new category of ad is growing more popular. I call them 'promotionals.' Like direct marketing, they have several pieces to them. There's a call to action, which could be a banner, an icon, whatever. Then there are jump pages, or microsites, that are attached to the call to action. Here we find the interactive component—a game to draw people in, or coupons that are sent to a viewer who registers."

WHAT'S YOUR CTR?

When business owners and media managers assess online advertising, most focus on the click-through rate, or CTR, which refers to the number of people who see an online ad and respond by clicking through to a Web site. How reliable are CTRs?

The fact is, all too many sites, even those that have a high click-through rate, are not receiving the response rates from banner ads their owners had hoped for. While the click-through rate tracks the number of times a viewer clicks on a banner ad and reaches the site, it does not measure the number of interested prospects or sales that come from an ad. In the end, it is not even sales (either online or off) that determine the success of any advertising campaign; it is revenue. That should be no different on the Web. If you have an inexpensive offering, perhaps an online service one can receive for, say, $5 a month, you need a high number of subscriptions to make the effort worthwhile. You'll need a high click-through rate, but more importantly you'll need to achieve certain revenue figures. If you sell a product for $200, you'll be satisfied with a much lower CTR, provided you are receiving the number of sales your projections indicate you need to run your business profitability. In either case, therefore, it is the revenue received that dictates the success of the ad.

This doesn't mean, however, that click-through rates are meaningless. Consider for a minute a company whose advertising attracts a high CTR, but whose resulting sales are not meeting projections. The disparity between CTR and revenue can indicate several potential problems. Most typically, these problems fall into one of two categories:

1. The Web site does not deliver on the promise of the advertising. The ad may build interest, but the site falls short. If this is the case, the site owner should evaluate the site carefully and ask the following questions:

- Does the banner ad click through to the offer or does it deposit prospective customers on the home page and require them to find the offer on their own?

- Is there enough information and supporting material to close the sale that the ad started?

- Is it easy to close the sale once the prospect arrives on the site? Studies show, for example, that if customers cannot use a credit card and order quickly and easily, they are likely to lose interest.

2. The banner ad is making an effective pitch, but it's the wrong pitch, given what the company has to sell. Even if your Web site is effective, if the message of an ad does not accurately reflect the item you are selling, you'll end up with disappointed prospects. In this case, people are clicking on the banner because they are attracted to its message, but the message is off-target. Web users are not stupid, and they do not appreciate being surprised or, worse, tricked.

On the other hand, when a product or service appears to be selling well and first-time visitors return to a site regularly but the traffic is not coming from banners, you have a different problem. The click-through rate is low because the banner ad is not promoting the message effectively. If there is a free offer, a special, low online price, or other added value, this needs to be spelled out in the banner ad. Spend some time looking at other companies' ads and you'll be surprised to discover how many of them focus on the company rather than on the specific product or offer. Banner advertising is not the place to build your company's image. It should be reserved for promoting specific offers available online.

ADVERTISING THAT BOOSTS RESPONSE

Like any form of advertising, there are techniques that work in banner ads and others that should be avoided at all cost. If you are ready to try banner advertising and want to get the most for your investment, here are some tested techniques you should consider:

- *Change the creative appeal often.* Most traditional advertising professionals say that clients tend to pull their ads and develop new creative appeals before they have gained the maximum return on investment. What happens is that the business owners, management, staff, and even their families have a heightened awareness of their own advertising. As you might expect, the ad breaks through the clutter and registers with them every time they see or hear it. This is not the case with the general public. They lack the predisposition of someone connected with the company or product. As a result, the company pulls the ad before it has had a chance to break through to the public.

  Alas, Web-based advertisers who have learned this lesson must unlearn it online. Experts suggest that people who see a banner ad online and respond favorably will click through to the site. The next time they see the ad, they will not respond. The difference lies in the fact that the Web provides instant response. You see the ad, it attracts you, and you click on it. Users don't bookmark banner ads. Given the randomness of their appearance, users know they had better click through when they see the ad. Who knows where or when they'll see the ad again? The "been there, done that" nature of Web-based advertising means you'll need to change ads much more often.

- *Pictures on banner ads do not have the same impact they have in print.* Banner ads are small, just a narrow strip running across the screen. Most images end up taking up too much room, leaving little space for the message. Thus, a graphic-intensive banner typically lacks focus or selling power. There's no room for the power words: free, lowest-price, limited time, act now, and so on. This is not to say a banner should not have graphic appeal, but graphics can't be used at the expense of your message.

- *Appeal to many senses.* Having said that graphics must be used with caution, many advertisers find success using movement, interactivity, and sound. Animation has been estimated by some to raise response rates by as much as 35 percent.

- *Test and test often.* To rate the effectiveness of any form of marketing or advertising, you need to test it. Advertising on the Web is no different, except that it is actually easier and more cost-effective to test online. For one thing, in this computerized environment, tracking results can be automated easily. Second, ads can be changed just as often and as quickly as they are generated. You don't have to wait for the next print cycle.

- *Bigger is better...at least to a degree.* It stands to reason that a larger, wider banner will attract more attention than a smaller one. One thing to keep in mind, though, is that as your ad becomes bigger, your file size can get out of hand. Try to keep the file size to 10K or 15K; otherwise the ad could take too long to load. Your audience will have moved on before your ad appears.

- *Create a call to action.* Just as we are told to include phrases like "Call now" and "Order today" in traditional advertising, we should do the same online. The difference is that online our call to action is "Click here" or "Visit our site now."

- *Remember the power words.* Because banners don't have space for a long message, you need to choose your words carefully. Several of the obvious words to include (if they apply) are "Free," "Limited offer," "New and improved." There are also a few that are unique to the Web: "Free download," "Personalized consultation," "Immediate response."

- *Don't blend into the background.* Stand out. Use bold colors that pull the eye.

- *Match advertising to your target market.* Whether in the message, the images, or the nature of the offer, remember your target market. Design an ad that appeals to the interests and age group of the customer you want to reach. If your product has wide appeal, then consider the site(s) you have selected to post your ad. If you place your ad on a site that attracts children make sure it is appropriate.

- *Location is critical.* Pick sites to run your ad that have strong numbers and attract your target market.

- *Don't resort to tricks.* If you pay attention to banners, you'll notice more and more that seem to look like part of the Web site. They have scroll bars and other devices that make them look like content. They often receive high CTRs, but beware. People who click on them unknowingly are often annoyed by the deception. You may get more people to your site, but you'll probably have a hard time keeping them. Worse, they will often leave angry.

EXCHANGE NETWORKS

Exchange networks are groups of Web sites that trade links and banners with each other. Typically, you'll create a space on your Web site to display the group's banner (which is served from their server, not yours) and in exchange, your banner (which you submit to them only once) will be displayed on other members' sites.

Exchanges are a great way to get started in banner advertising (and they're free!). The exchange you join will provide the necessary HTML code for you to place on your site. All you have to do is sign up and provide them with a banner for your site. Here are two exchange networks to consider:

- LinkExchange: This is the largest banner-swapping (reciprocal advertising) network. Open to anyone, it currently has more than a million members. You display two banners on your site in exchange for having your banner displayed once on other members' sites. This is a professionally run, excellent service.

- IntelliClick: The first free banner exchange network to offer the ability to include sound effects with your banner ad (no plug-ins required).

VIABLE ALTERNATIVES TO BANNER ADS

With click-through rates often at less than 2 percent, what are some alternatives to banner advertising for Web sites? There are more than you might think. The banner may get a lot of press attention and it may be the most common form of Web site advertising, but it is not the only option for advertising your Web site on the Internet.

Let's take a look at several other Net advertising techniques that are gaining popularity.

Badges and buttons. Badges are small graphics that can be seen in many places where a full-size banner ad wouldn't fit or wouldn't be appropriate. Take a look at Newslinx, at www.newslinx.com. Scroll down the page and you'll see a badge for TechTalk, an Internet radio show.

One of the benefits of badges is that they can be placed in so many locations on a site, while most full-size banners are placed at the top of the page only. Also, badges are often less expensive on a cost-per-thousand basis than banners and can be negotiated as to price and location in many more ways than traditional banners. The same goes for a button, which is a variation of a badge.

Take a look at the bottom of the page at www.yahoo.com to see a button. Smaller than a badge, this button features a Visa logo that jumps out more than you would expect. Note that in this case the button is augmented by a small bit of text that says "Smart Shopping With," just before the button. Some people use the terms *badge* and *button* interchangeably, and this is fine. The concept is what's most important, because the advertiser doesn't have to be boxed into a banner ad as the only option.

These types of ad options are available to you, though you may need to ask for them.

A buy in action. To see a key word buy in action, go back to Yahoo! and do a search on the term "office supplies." The page of results that comes up has a banner ad for Quill Office Products above the search results. Quill paid Yahoo for the key words "office supplies," so when a user searches with that term, the Quill banner is displayed—a nice targeting method that often results in better click-through rates.

Interstitial ads. Moving further still from the banner ad is the interstitial. One type of interstitial ad is a marketing message included between two pages of a site. Put simply, it's a message that comes after the page you were just on and before the page you are waiting to see. Some studies indicate these types of ads are more effective than any other type of Web ad. Another type of interstitial is a new browser window that appears the moment a link is clicked, so that two browser windows are open on the user's screen. Some users, including me, find this approach irritating, while others like it.

Using a microsite. Microsites are often used on corporate intranets and work something like this: Suppose a corporation has a regular need to deliver products within a certain geographic region, and it uses any one of several delivery services. One of the delivery services builds a 10-page Web site, with a full set of services and pricing and an online booking feature. It then offers to house this microsite on the corporation's intranet, making it easier for the corporation's employees to access and book deliveries. If this isn't feasible, then the service houses the microsite at a password-protected URL given out only to the corporation's users. This microsite is separate from the service's main company site. In fact, the company could build as many microsites as it wished.

BUSINESS-TO-BUSINESS BANNERS

While consumer companies have long dominated the Web banner business, advertisers targeting other businesses are now getting into the game. They face two key issues: using rich media tools effectively to draw in users, and discovering the best placement for their banners. Often, the key to capturing the attention of online business users lies in adding an element of interactivity that plain animated banners simply can't offer.

The truth is, new Web advertising and marketing techniques are being developed every day. The banner ad caught on, but it may well end up as one of the least effective of all options.

BANNER STANDARDS

The Standards and Practices Committee of the IAB (International Advertising Bureau) has used market data to examine the full range of banner types (vertical, horizontal, half, and button) and sizes currently in use. The Committee has identified the following as the most commonly accepted:

Size (pixels):	Type:
468 × 60	Full Banner
234 × 60	Half Banner
392 × 72	Full Banner with Vertical Navigation Bar
120 × 240	Vertical Banner
125 × 125	Square Button
120 × 90	Button #1
120 × 60	Button #2
88 × 31	Micro Button

ONLINE MEDIA KIT DEVELOPMENT

While much of the focus here has been on how to make your own advertising more effective, you may also want to take steps to attract advertisers to your site. Now you can sell ads all day and all night, seven days a week, without ever leaving your office. The fact is, developing an online media kit is the smartest investment you can make. Putting your media kit online will give you:

- *Extended visibility:* With the click of a mouse, your advertisers can access rates, demographics, circulation, editorial calendars, phone and FAX numbers, and more at any hour of the day or night. Whenever media decisions are made, your information will be available.

- *The opportunity to open two-way e-mail communications* with anyone visiting your site. Advertisers can e-mail you to request more information or a personal call from an account executive . . . and you'll get their names and addresses to conduct cost-effective e-mail promotions of your own.

- *Flexibility:* You can revise your media kit pages overnight, so your advertisers always get the most up-to-date information available.

- *Savings in time and money:* You'll use fewer faxes and messengers.

AN ENVIRONMENT FOR TESTING

I can't stress enough the need to test both marketing and advertising messages and tactics. Even the best-conceived plans can fail. Even if they don't fail, how will you know whether you can improve the response rate unless you test and track the results? Don't ever be satisfied. You can always improve the draw. Here are a few ideas to test in your own campaigns:

- *Test your words.* Are you being clear? Are you attracting prospects who match your ideal demographics?

- *Test a variety of sites,* with variations in demographics and traffic, to determine which ones deliver the most and the best prospects.

- *Set up mirror sites to track every advertisement separately* to find out where you're making money and where you are not. Then you can maximize your profits by canceling the ads that don't work and maximizing the ads that do. Doing this is critical!

- *Test the location of your advertisement.* Try different placements on the page and a variety of sites.

- *Advertise through e-mail*, but only to those who have agreed to receive promotions.

  - Make the copy short and compelling.

  - Offer something (information, service, special pricing, newletter).

  - Introduce new products first, and at introductory prices.

- *Consider the value of follow-up e-mail.* When someone buys, send him or her a second offer through e-mail. Each opportunity to correspond should be viewed as a new opportunity to sell.

Cost-Effective Measurement

CASIE is a joint project of the Association of National Advertisers, Inc. and the American Association of Advertising Agencies. With the support of the Advertising Research Foundation (ARF), CASIE has created the Guiding Principles of Interactive Media Audience Measurement, supplying guidelines for providing quality audience measurement of interactive media. They are summarized on the following page.

In order for a new medium to develop as an advertising vehicle, it must be able to offer the industry both acceptable measures of the opportunities it delivers and the means to compare it to existing alternatives. It is the intent of these principles to provide the foundation for the accurate and reliable research needed to meet both requirements.

These principles are offered to interactive media and research providers to help them mutually invest their efforts and capital in developing audience measurement systems for the interactive media environment. The principles may be used by industry to help evaluate new audience measurement research efforts, and by advertisers to help make intelligent investment decisions about interactive media opportunities. Here are a few issues to consider:

- *Third-Party Measurement or Auditing:* Audience measurements should be taken by objective third-party research suppliers and not by the medium being measured. Measurement by the medium itself via the clickstream, when offered, should be audited by an objective third party. In all cases, established industry auditing practices should be employed. Third-party audience measurement could also benefit from being audited.

- *Full Disclosure:* Complete information about the research methods and practices used, as well as all the data collected, should be revealed to all research subscribers. Carefully scrutinized exceptions may be made so as to allow research providers to protect trade secrets, when the claim of such trade secrets preventing the disclosure of specific information is judged to be credible by the user community based on the known facts of the specific case.

- *Comparability:* It is highly desirable that audience estimates covering a particular interactive vehicle be directly comparable to estimates covering another interactive vehicle within the same interactive medium.

- *Methodological Experimentation Encouraged:* Research organizations are encouraged to be innovative in method and practice. The burden of proof of the validity of the measurement and of conclusions based on the measurement is on the research company.

- *User Information Preferable:* To evaluate audiences of a medium, advertisers need to know the number of different users accessing the medium and the number of times they access it in a given period of time. The product of these two key measures provides a gross exposures measure (called "visits" in cyberspace) that can be used to calculate measures of cost-efficiency comparable to other media. Together, these key measures provide data comparable to that available for other media.

- *Use of Census and Sample:* Measurement of users at the level of persons rather than households may, in many cases, necessitate the use of a sample. While a census has advantages over a sample, the need for a measurement of individual person users should not be compromised in order to gain these advantages. When and if a truly complete and accurate census of users is made available, that is most preferable. A combination of a census of visits plus a users' sample is one viable approach to maximizing accuracy at every level.

- *Nonintrusiveness:* Measurement methods that are least visible to consumers and require the least effort on their part are preferable to methods that are more visible to consumers or that require more effort.

- *Total Medium Measurement:* It is highly desirable that audience estimates be provided within the context of a total medium measurement, so that principal vehicles within that medium might be directly evaluated against one another and against the total medium norms.

- *Industry Consensus:* Interactive media research standards ought to be set by a broad representation of the advertising industry, including advertisers, agencies, media, research companies, and industry bodies.

Hits are the least desirable level at which to measure cyberspace media, because hits do not provide a constant yardstick for all Web pages. The fact that the hits measure evolved from within the cyberspace community without consultation with the advertising industry and is at cross-purposes to the need of cyberspace media to secure advertising revenues underscores the need for the present effort represented by this document.

Pages are an acceptable ancillary measurement level, but should not be considered a replacement for visits, users, and identified users. However, it is highly desirable that acceptable audience measures be taken and reported at the level of discrete content elements whenever possible so that advertising content may be measured directly and not imputed from surrounding editorial content.

In summary, there are a great many ways to get the word out about your site. But keep in mind that advertising is only half the work of having a successful site. The other half is creating a site that is informative and engaging and makes visitors want to return or tell their friends. Like any traditional promotion or advertising, your efforts can only bring people to your site. You still need to maintain a site that meets the needs of your prospective customers. Don't disappoint them. Deliver what you promise.

E-BUSINESS: THE REAL ADVANTAGE

Whether business-to-consumer or business-to-business, most business owners tend to focus on the e-commerce aspects of the Internet. But when you consider some of the models Web-based businesses are creating—namely, to gain members and site visitors at all cost—the prospect of earning a satisfactory return online may be discouraging. The drive to build a critical mass of users is behind strategies to sell products at cost, with the hope of making up the difference in advertising revenues.

This model will probably change, particularly if advertising becomes less confined to a relative handful of major players and portal sites. As Web-based businesses continue to go public in the hope of earning large influxes of capital, the day will come when investors will demand real returns on their investments. This, perhaps more than anything, will force the change. To meet investor expectations, companies will need to earn revenue on products as well as on advertising.

Regardless of the eventual outcome, it is clear that the greatest advantage the Internet provides to every business, small and large, is the ability to conduct e-business. E-business includes the applications companies can apply to their businesses to help them communicate more effectively with employees, customers, and suppliers. It includes online systems and services that help business owners automate complex tasks, including supply chain management and all the management methods yet to be invented. And it includes the easy access in-house and on the road that might be cost-prohibitive to install on a network based in the home office.

Just as e-commerce is proving a powerful tool for the owners of small businesses by enabling them to compete in markets around the world that appeared off-limits just a few years ago, so e-business will greatly benefit the small business owner. For one thing, it provides access to applications the small business owner could never afford to own outright. Online, these tools are available as services. Management signs up for as much or as little service as it wants or needs.

It's understandable that much of the industry focus has been on the growth of e-commerce, both the increasing comfort of customers with online transactions and the growing number of businesses selling over the Web. In the long run, however, the broader category of e-business will probably have the greatest impact on the way companies do business. Rather than a source of revenue, e-business represents a major source of savings, which ultimately impacts the bottom line as directly. Furthermore, the automation it offers for many systems and processes that are still performed manually in small firms provides a boost in productivity that has long been the promise of technology. The WorkSafe System is just one example.

The WorkSafe System (www.worksafesystem.com), developed by Safety Management Corporation and Integrated Corporate Solutions Inc., is an outgrowth of two popular programs—WorkSafe and EnvironSafe—that help companies in many industries manage OSHA- and EPA-compliant environmental, health, and safety programs for their employees. The way the online service operates clearly demonstrates the potential for e-business solutions. In short, simple, and powerful and can be cost-effective.

Without having to install or upgrade software, maintain a server, or support and manage a system, companies can subscribe to a comprehensive service designed to help them satisfy government requirements. The solution, built using Lotus®Domino™ and hosted on the IBM Global Network™, handles system security, capacity planning, system management, and performance tuning. It provides a cost-effective solution designed to make companies' workplace environments safer, while minimizing their exposure to OSHA and EPA fines and penalties. As a result, subscribers may be able to:

- Reduce workers' compensation premiums.
- Face fewer liability claims filed by employees.
- Increase productivity in the workplace.
- Reduce their investment in technology and its service and support.

While the WorkSafe System does not bring in additional customer revenue, there may be dollars saved through better administration and lower costs resulting from a safer, more compliant workplace that will impact the bottom line directly.

BUILDING AN INTRANET

Company intranets—internal networks running on the Internet—are fast becoming useful environments for sharing product information, handling order-taking tasks, and encouraging companywide discussion. Because it streamlines the fulfillment and delivery process through the company, it's a more efficient means of buying and receiving, and gives purchasing departments faster and more up-to-date access to offerings in our "I need it yesterday" world.

Phase 2 Development is a fast-growing networking and Internet product company. Its revenues rose 800 percent in one year, and in the span of about 14 months it grew from 9 employees to 65. Because not all the employees are located in the same place, they needed a powerful means of internal communication. They chose to build an intranet—a companywide network for employees that resides on the Internet.

The Phase 2 Development's intranet solves several problems and reduces bottlenecks for the company. For example, they use their site to compress the sales cycle through electronic communications. Mark Towler calls it "virtual engineering." Information is shared electronically among engineers, designers, artists, and programmers who can all work on a project at the same time and share their work online. "Today a global team can do things simultaneously and network their human intelligence to get to the answers a lot quicker," Towler explains. "Rather than waiting until one group has finished before the next can start, teams can process ideas and work in parallel."

Human resource planning is a big job for a fast-growing company. But with the intranet, new employees don't have to wait for HR people to talk with them. They just enter the company Web site and, through internal communications, learn about their 401k plan, the employee manual, or policies and procedures. The company avoids printing and distributing big packages of benefits information. For example, employees can sign up for a plan and pick the mutual funds for their 401k. The forms go directly to the outside firm handling the 401k, and any questions not answered on the site can be answered directly by the provider by a phone call. Health care enrollment is handled the same way. In a few years, Phase 2 Development hopes to have several hundred employees in different geographical locations. "When that happens," adds Towler, "we won't have a beast of an HR department."

The intranet is also reducing internal costs. In a traditional business, the manager of administration could be on the phone all day and still not answer all employee questions. There is no time left for strategic planning. Administrators are important, but their time can't be billed, so the only way to reduce costs is to keep administration as small as possible. Intranet communication lets companies do the most with the least head count. Towler outsourced much of the specialized administrative expertise needed, rather than hiring it; all the outside firm had to do was adjust to the company's need to communicate electronically.

MARK TOWLER ON E-BUSINESS

The world is obviously rapidly moving to a network world. The important thing for the small businessperson to understand is that the computer is not what's on your desktop; the computer is the network. Your desktop is only as powerful and robust as the network that it's hooked up to.

What's the most powerful network out there on the planet? The Internet. So the question becomes, in my mind, what is networking all about? And what leverage does a small businessperson gain by tapping into the resources of the network?

The key is networking your intelligence. What you really do through digital technology is network your intelligence, not network computers. The small businessperson needs to learn how to align this intelligence network with his or her business objectives. Whatever those business objectives are, especially in a small business, it is the power of the network that will separate the haves from the have-nots ten years from now.

A lot of what we do is architecture. We engineer and design networked, integrated solutions to meet those business objectives. And we support them and host them on server farms, where we have Web sites going out to the Internet.

In a small business, your biggest asset is your human intelligence—not the computers, not the products. And how do you leverage that? Through technology. The Internet is unbelievable! It's really a powerful, powerful technology.

Our target market is companies in the $10 million to $500 million revenue range that have growth agendas and understand that they need to use technology as a vehicle for growth. We try to help them understand that using technology is not buying computers for the sake of buying computers; it's designing an info technology solution that meets your business *objectives, fits the culture of your organization, and can fit into your overall business plan. We go in and design an info technology solution to meet your business objectives, just as architects would do in planning to build a large property.*

I don't care if your revenues are $10 million or $200 million. I think you would be surprised to see that you don't really have an information technology architecture, a strategic plan that aligns with your business objectives. I think that in the information technology business, the problem has historically been that the services providers have done a lousy job of promoting themselves as professional partners, like, for example, your audit firm or your attorney or your banker. And I think that in the twenty-first century the technology partner may still not elevate itself to that status, but that is our goal. The technology partner helps you to achieve your objectives much as the other professionals do.

When I speak to businesspeople I say, Try to picture an organization that is networking its people through technology, that is responding to clients quickly, that is getting to the market quickly, and that is having fun but achieving objectives and doing it profitably. Then picture that organization as your competitor.

That should be a motivator. Road kill is probably a severe term, but I think it represents how we are going to see some companies that cannot understand how to develop a competitive advantage and really secure their niche. Technology can change the business you are in. It certainly changes the competitive landscape very quickly. Look at the companies that were on the Fortune 500 thirty years ago; only a very small percentage of them are left.

I would argue that that is due to the advent of technology. Change is the number one, big time, big dog, very scary hurdle. You may think that all of what I said sounds good, but the execution of it is a big challenge. Take any function or process in a business—order processing, for example— and you have employees who have been doing it the same way for fifteen years, with a telephone and a pad of paper, maybe even with a PC. Now they are asked to begin to do it on a network, and their response is, "No. We have done it this way for fifteen years, and it's worked."

To young companies, this is no big deal. We are very fortunate in that we are a young company. But we have customers that don't have that advantage. For companies that are thirty to forty years old, trying to implement technology initiatives can be a painful process. It can rip the heart out of your organization if you are not careful to plan and promote it correctly.

The ability to speak electronically is another concept I try to promote, especially in smaller organizations. I don't know how many e-mails a day fly through here—thousands. That is because we are trying to leverage our intelligence quickly and to respond to the market quickly.

I believe that the impact of electronic language on our society will be the same as spoken language, written language, and printed language. Think of the impact these modes of language had on society. They changed the landscape. What's amazing to me is that anybody else can do it. We know our prospect pretty well before we go in, and we have mocked up some solutions. It's all online. We do all of our presentations on the Web, for both prospects and clients.

A lot of what we do is using the Web as a front end to tie into a back end application. So typically our work is not just an electronic brochure. There's a business application, done with some creativity in terms of whatever the application.

For example, suppose we need to do a mock-up for a Web site. The client e-mails us some graphics. All our people aren't in the same office; it's all shared and spun up electronically between one of our info technology engineers and an original artist and a Web master and a programmer. And it's all done online so that development work is all done simultaneously, the way you might have a graphic artist work on the artwork.

CONCLUSION

P redicting what to expect next of the Internet is akin to viewing a crystal ball or reading tea leaves, but not for the same reasons. A fortuneteller relies on unknown, unseen extrasensory powers. With the Internet, we have tangibles on which to base our opinions. The problem is that we also have a history of tradition. Our views of the future often are products of what we have seen and experienced in the past.

Mention to anyone that shopping malls and local retailers might disappear into cyberspace, and wait for the reaction. Few can imagine such a world. "I need to see and touch the items I'm planning to buy," is one response I've heard more than once. "I like to go to the mall and be around people," is another typical reply. But if our shopping centers did disappear, who is to say that something new and exciting would not provide the entertainment and social interaction we crave? Consider too that a generation growing up with video games and virtual reality may not feel the same need to touch and see before purchasing.

It's not easy to predict precisely where the Internet will lead us. And yet, trends that have taken shape during the past decade provide, at least, a place to start. As a business owner, you need to envision the future of the Internet in terms of its impact on business. Here are a few of the trends we might expect to see in the future:

Faster access. Between technological breakthroughs, continued merging of cable, phone, and wireless firms and their technologies, and increased access to broadband communications, we can expect that users at home and office will experience faster online access and download times. This will result in the greater integration of large graphics, video, and audio without losing prospective customers to long download times. Internet sites and advertising will provide a sensory experience not unlike television.

Greater integration of technologies. This, to a large extent, goes hand in hand with the previous expectation. But let's go a step farther. Only a few years ago, we thought of microchips as the heart and brains of our computers. Today we realize that they also control most of the electronics in our household and office appliances. Computer technology is part of our lives, whether or not we use a laptop or desktop system. The same is true of communication technologies. They will come together under the Internet banner. Concepts like Web TV and set-top cable boxes providing Internet access are just the beginning. We still think of communication and computing as two distinct technologies. In fact, they will become one. Television will have the interactive powers of the Internet and the Internet will have the real-time speeds of television. And technology will go farther, to include radio, telephone, and more. Companies are already offering low-priced long-distance calling via the Web, and video conferencing can be carried on over the Web. Just as we manage our e-mail and schedules via the Internet, we'll manage our smart homes and businesses online.

Increased emphasis on privacy. Privacy has been a mainstream issue for decades, gaining public awareness with the Presidential Commission on

Privacy in the 1970s. To date, most industries have been self-regulating. If Internet-based businesses and technology firms demonstrate their commitment, they too will probably remain largely self-regulating. But the Internet does amplify the potential problems and abuses, making privacy an issue that deserves head-on confrontation. If the proper steps are not taken, an already concerned public will respond by closing their pocketbooks and refusing to provide personal information. They will, in large part, shut down the growth of e-commerce and destroy the real benefits—to both consumers and companies—of data mining. If the potential of e-commerce is used responsibly, we will all benefit from an increasingly personalized experience online.

Demographics that more closely mirror populations worldwide. Increased bandwidth worldwide and the dissolution of government regulations are enabling more people of the world to enjoy the communication and commercial benefits of the Internet. This will open the world to global business, presenting both opportunity and increased competition. We can already see this trend emerging. The year 1999 was expected to be the breakthrough year, when the United States would no longer represent the majority online. In the United States, more women were expected to be online than men. Lower access costs and more public access to the Internet through libraries, schools, and community centers is giving people of all economic backgrounds an opportunity to use the services and information available online.

Strong and pervasive security, resulting in reduced fears. Security will always be an issue. Anything we can build, someone else can eventually break. Although security breaches will never disappear entirely, new technology is making the threat manageable. New, more powerful algorithms make secure software applications better, and smart-card technology (already built into Windows and available in limited online applications) will provide a physical deterrent that will be harder to breach. Surveys responses naming security as one of the primary reasons for not conducting transactions online will decline. Another issue that will probably not disappear as easily concerns the fact that most security breaches are internal—perpetrated by disgruntled or unethical employees. Companies have been slower to build security into their internal systems. This is an area that businesses large and small need to respond to.

Pervasive use of the Internet. Today we think of accessing the Internet at home or at the office. When we are on the road, we can gain access via a modem connected to a hotel phone or, in some cases, through our cellular phones. Personal digital assistants, such as IBM's WorkPad, provide more flexible access. Pagers and cellular phones also provide access. This is just the beginning. Most experts believe that in the near future, we will have access from virtually anywhere. Stores are installing kiosks with access to their Web sites from the store. New devices will soon make gaining Internet access as simple as turning on a handheld video game system or turning on an automobile. The result will be an expectation of information and services that will help us in many ways—online directions to a destination, quick currency converters, language translation systems, and so on. Many of these already exist; our reliance on them will only grow.

Greater expectation of transacting payments online. While the number of sites (even e-commerce sites) that support secure, online payment systems is still in the minority, this will change. The change will be a result of the greater security measures already mentioned, but also the result of an increasing level of comfort and expectation on the part of the public. Buyers will gravitate to sites that support and facilitate online purchasing.

More competition. Between the global deluge of Internet users and the increasing pervasiveness of businesses and homes online, worldwide competition will increase. The longer businesses wait to get online, become established, and learn the ins and outs of what works online, the farther behind they will become. An iCat Corporation survey shows that 28 percent of small business say they face online competition today, and 62 percent expect rivals to appear within the next five years.

With the rate of acceptance by businesses and the wild enthusiasm investors have shown for Internet IPOs, it's hard to imagine business without the Web. The competition will result in several scenarios: greater imagination directed toward Web site design; new services; and better, more targeted marketing. Business owners need to be prepared for the inevitable. Furthermore, they must understand that the act of getting online is only the first step. Achieving success online demands a continuous effort.

Shareholder expectations of real profits. The excitement and acceptance investors have shown Internet-based businesses and their unconventional business models and strategies to attract consumers will wear thin—unless the payoff is real. In fact, only a handful of very aggressive businesses are throwing away all the conventions of commerce to quickly attract millions of names and members that they hope to leverage for sales and advertising revenue. There is no question that the Internet has helped to usher in a new generation of business, and many of the old theories must be put aside. How much business will really change is still unknown. In the meantime, business owners need to evaluate new strategies and tactics carefully and weigh them against practices that are working today. As we've indicated in these pages, many e-businesses are realizing profits today (although still a small percentage of their total revenue). As time goes on, stockholders in these wildly successful IPOs will hold management accountable for delivering operating profits.

Leveling of prices online and offline. A study by the University of Pennsylvania's Wharton School suggests that pricing online is not always clearly the lowest. Using 1997 data, they found a 20 percent variance among the prices of airline tickets sold online. If you listen to the reports of those who frequent the online auctions, you will hear complaints of items selling for much more than their estimated value. Auction fever apparently takes over, and pushes bidding prices higher than retail.

More emphasis on e-business. Whether or not a company engages in e-commerce transactions, there is much to gain from e-business. The dollar savings, increased productivity, accuracy, and reduced need for staff all have a dramatic impact on the bottom line. Services that provide consumers and business owners with the benefits of e-business will be big winners. Don't overlook savings when calculating the value of the Internet to you or your customers.

Continued strength of business-to-business sites. Consumer applications and sites may get most of the press, but business-to-business is (and will continue to be) the mainstay of the Internet. If you have products or services aimed at the business market, cultivate the Internet now. You have access to a market that will demonstrate significant returns for many years to come.

Broader base of consumer goods available for sale online. Much of the focus of online buying has been on books, software, computer equipment, apparel, travel, and music. But this is only the beginning. If you have an unexplored niche, you may find a strong market online. Given the number of businesses already entrenched in today's popular market categories, niches represent new opportunities your prospective customers may be eager to explore.

Increasing customer expectations for convenience, ease-of-use, and efficiency. Value will continue to be important to Internet users. This, after all, helps distinguish Web-based commerce and services from their more traditional competition. Why do business online when there are stores and businesses a short drive away? Online businesses must offer new value, better service, and greater convenience and ease of use than are otherwise available.

Customer service as an imperative. During the 1999 Christmas season, online sales more than doubled over the previous year. While this was good news for e-commerce advocates (and a wake-up call for traditional retailers), many Web-based businesses found their systems overtaxed. For all the benefits of shopping online and avoiding the crowded mall, customer service remains high in customers' minds. They require good return policies, easy access to help, and understanding…lots of understanding. The smartest online business owners are taking advantage of the Internet to provide greater (more cost-effective) service than they could afford or justify using traditional systems and technology. Don't overlook customer service.

It's impossible to know exactly what the future will bring. I suggest only that what we imagine is probably only the tip of the iceberg. The Internet will continue to usher in tremendous change. All you can do is keep current. Watch the competition. Keep your imagination and creativity set on high. And don't be reined in by the past.

On his personal Web site, IBM CEO and chairman Louis Gerstner writes: "Every day it becomes more clear that the Net is taking its place alongside the other great transformational technologies that first challenged, and then fundamentally changed, the way things are done in the world. Certainly the Net is a powerful medium for communication. But even more important, it is a vocational medium—a place where real work gets done, real competitive advantage is gained, and real growth is generated."

Our hope is that this book will help you realize your dreams and potential online—and enjoy the experience along the way. Above all, by committing to the Internet, you are starting out on a journey that will take you and your business beyond your imagination. There is no end point, just growth and more opportunity.

GLOSSARY

Banner Short for "banner advertisement," a graphic or image used for advertising on the Internet.

Browser The software program an individual uses to navigate through the World Wide Web. Some popular browsers are Netscape, Mosaic, and Internet Explorer. The features of a particular browser, such as on-screen menus, set the tone for a user's Web experience.

CGI (Common Gateway Interface) Programs allowing interaction (e-mail inquiries, job applications, order forms, etc.) on the Web. Interfaces are written in computer languages such as perl or C++.

Clicks or Click-Throughs The number of times an ad has been clicked by visitors. A measure of response.

CMC (Computer-Mediated Communications) CMC is how telephones and computers have evolved into a system whereby virtually all communications occurs first via computers establishing links; this includes voice conversations. The worldwide telecommunications network links computers in virtually every community in the world to other computers, and the network that carries our voices can also carry computer-to-computer communications.

CPM Cost per thousand impressions. A way to price banner ads. If an advertiser's CPM is $25, then you get 1,000 impressions of your banner on his or her site for $25.

CTR Click-through ratio. A method of rating how many times a banner is clicked on. A ratio of the number of times a banner is shown to the number of times it is clicked on. For example, if a banner has a CTR of 20:1, it means that 1 out of 20 people have clicked on it (i.e., 5% of the people who viewed it).

Cyberspace A term coined originally by science fiction writer William Gibson (in the book *Neuromancer*), now used to describe the "space" where words, relationships, information, and money exist with computer-mediated communications; otherwise known as the Information Highway.

DNS (Domain Name System) A method used by the Internet to assign addresses to computers. This helps people e-mail information successfully from point A to point B. Your domain name is the name by which you will be internationally known and accessed on the Internet. Examples: nando.net, aol.com, unc.edu.

E-Mail (Electronic Mail) Mail delivered electronically. You use electronic mail programs to compose, send, and receive messages or files with other people who also have e-mail addresses.

Encryption A process that enables sensitive material to be transmitted with min-

253

imal risk of access by unwanted parties, often used for banking information or military messages.

FTP (File Transfer Protocol) An Internet application that lets you transfer files, including photographs and computer software, from a remote computer to your personal computer.

GIF Graphic Interchange Format. A common file format for Web graphics (and banners). Not always the best choice for photo-realistic images.

Hit A questionable measure of Web site traffic. Counts one hit each time a browser request is made from a Web server. For example, a page containing 5 images counts 6 hits each time it is viewed (one for each image and one for the page itself). *Page views* provide a much better way to measure traffic.

Homepage Your initial interface to the Web and the many documents, files, and resources that reside on it. It is also the first document a company wants a new user to see when first going to its Web site, as it contains links to various other Web pages of information offered by the company.

HTML (Hypertext Markup Language) The coding language used to put text and graphics together to create Web pages. It is the current language of the Web.

Hypertext Computer-based electronic documents that use hyperlinks to link pages to other sites, databases, graphics, stories, etc., enabling users to follow a line of thought by "clicking" on a word.

Impression A measure of how many times a banner is displayed. Counts one impression each time the banner is shown.

Interactive A term used to describe Web communication. Your Web page is interactive if it allows a user to both submit and request information from your company via the Web server.

Java A programming language that supports animation and real-time information delivery.

JPG (or JPEG) Joint Photographic Experts Group. A common file format for photo-realistic images. Not as common as GIF for banners, because JPEG compression has a tendency to blur small text (which banners usually contain).

Link An image on a sponsorable site that functions as a link to another company's site.

Log File All raw hits to a Web server are recorded in this file. The log files are used to calculate and track usage and are later verified by third-party audit firms.

Page View A measure of how many times a complete page is displayed. Counts one page view each time a page is displayed.

Server A repository for Web documents. Your information must reside on at least one server on the Internet for other people to access it. Servers vary widely in features, popularity, and accessibility, which affects their associated costs and fees.

Telnet An Internet application that lets you connect to remote computers and run programs or browse through information.

URL (Uniform Resource Locator) The address at which your documents reside on the World Wide Web. Example: http://www.shopnow.com

Web Server The actual computer that stores all the files for a Web site.

WWW (World Wide Web) The emerging high end of the Internet that allows users to see pictures, hear sound, see video clips, and read hypertext documents, as well as link from document to document or one computer to another by simply clicking on choices that appear on the computer monitor. The Web allows users to communicate interactively with organizations, other users, and companies on the Internet. There is no central organization controlling the Web; rather, organizations and companies control their own participation by means of independent servers.

INDEX

255

ABOUT THE AUTHOR

Kendra R. Bonnett is former president of Mark Stevens &
Company and the founding editor of IBM's *Profit* magazine. She
has written articles for *Computer World*, *PC Week*, and the
web-related *IBM Business Connection*, and is the author of *The
Creative PrintMaster: Graphic Design Tips for Computer Users*.
She also authored two books for the editors of *Digit* magazine,
including *The Everyone Can Build a Robot Book*. She is
president of K-Vell Consulting in Greenwich, Connecticut.